a love that never lets go

by

Lisa Harper

Published by: LifeWay Press®
Nashville, TN

Published by LifeWay Press®
© 2012 • Lisa Harper
Third printing 2012

ISBN 978-1-4158-7234-5
Item 005474743

Dewey decimal classification: 231.6
Subject headings: GOD--MERCY \ BIBLE. O.T. MALACHI--STUDY \ LOVE

To order additional copies of this resource, write to LifeWay Church Resources Cus-
tomer Service; One LifeWay Plaza; Nashville, TN 37234-0113; fax (615) 251-5933;
phone (800) 458-2772; e-mail orderentry@lifeway.com; order online at www.lifeway.
com; or visit the LifeWay Christian Store serving you.

Printed in the United States of America

Adult Ministry Publishing
LifeWay Church Resources
One LifeWay Plaza
Nashville, TN 37234-0152

This Bible study is dedicated to my friend, Sabrina Webb, who is one of the kindest and bravest women I know. And to my precious mom, Patti Angel, who introduced me to Jesus.

No. 166181

Property of

....

....

....

ABOUT THE AUTHOR

Rarely are the terms hilarious storyteller and theological scholar used in the same sentence, much less used to describe the same person, but Lisa Harper is anything but stereotypical! She has been lauded as a master storyteller, whose writing and speaking overflows with colorful pop culture references that connect the dots between the Bible era and modern life.

Her vocational resume includes six years as the director of Focus on the Family's national women's ministry, followed by six years as the women's ministry director at a large church. Her academic resume includes a Master of Theological Studies with honors from Covenant Seminary. Now a sought-after Bible teacher and speaker, Lisa is currently featured on the national Women of Faith tour and speaks at many other large multi-denominational events—such as Kathy Trocoli's Among Friends, LifeWay's Abundance, and Women of Joy conferences—as well as at hundreds of churches all over the world. She's been on numerous syndicated radio and television programs and was featured on the cover of Today's Christian Woman.

She's written 10 books including *Stumbling Into Grace: Confessions of a Sometimes Spiritually Clumsy Woman* and *A Perfect Mess: Why You Don't Have to Worry About Being Good Enough For God*. Yet in spite of her credentials, the most noticeable thing about Lisa Harper is her authenticity. When asked about her accomplishments recently she said, "I'm so grateful for the opportunities God's given me; but don't forget, He often uses donkeys and rocks!"

contents

8   week 1.
when your tara's trashed (and your dog is dead)

28   week 2.
God's definitive declaration of affection

52   week 3.
going big or going home

80   week 4.
our Creator is a committed family man

104   week 5.
when divine grace masquerades as discipline

126   week 6.
God's miraculous return on our meager investments

148   week 7.
the promise of pirouetting livestock

174   closing the book of malachi

introduction & group suggestions

This past week at The Next Door (a residential recovery program for women), I noticed some of my girls seemed flustered as I began our session. As my mouth kept running, I wondered: *Have I said something shocking, confusing, or inappropriate?* One of the women graciously interrupted and said, "Lisa, your shirt's busted." I looked and the zipper on my hoodie had split apart, completely exposing me from neck to waist. Talk about letting it all hang out in Bible study!

After my laugh-inducing incident, our conversation took a more serious turn when I exposed a broken place in my heart. I confessed my complete exhaustion from the stress of trying to adopt a crack addict's baby, preparing for my dad's impending death from lung cancer, my mother's recent stage-four cancer diagnosis, and my crazy travel schedule. I didn't wrap my pain up in a spiritual metaphor or tie it up with an acrostic bow. I was too sad and tired to be "inspirational."

That's why I was so moved by what happened next. The newest member of our group—a precious young woman, released from a prison less than a week before—put her hand on my shoulder and prayed the Serenity Prayer. While she was praying, her voice caught with emotion and her face became wet with tears.

She was able to identify with my sorrow and fatigue because she knew what it felt like to be sad and tired. Her scars provided sanctity and empathy. When I walked out, my footsteps were both lighter and more purposeful. She reminded me that revealing our weaknesses against the backdrop of God's wondrous mercy encourages other limping sinners to stumble toward Jesus.

I pray that this Bible study becomes a safe place for you to let it all hang out too. Which means some days you might laugh until your sides ache. Other days you might cry until you're dehydrated. But I hope every day you get together with friends to explore God's immutable affection in Malachi will be a good day—that you'll walk a little lighter and closer to Jesus as a result.

We've created the format of *Malachi* to be liberating. Well, liberating for a Bible study anyway! Each week, we've included a 2-page viewer and group guide. Simply watch the video and use the discussion-starter questions to get everybody talking. The first session, you'll just watch the video and get to know each other. Then complete your study during the first week. When you get together for the second week, discuss the previous week's study.

We've segmented the book into chunks instead of days so you can complete it whenever you have time—like when the baby's sleeping, when your husband's glued to a football game on TV, or when you have the bathroom door locked and are hiding out from everybody. If you have one of those crazy-busy weeks, simply skim the key sections highlighted in the book and you won't feel like an unspiritual basket case during small-group time!

You'll notice the study looks like the manuscript for a play. We chose that motif because reading Malachi is kind of like perusing the script for a theater production. Instead of plain, straightforward text, Malachi presents his message in the form of dramatic dialogues with a cast of characters as colorful as a Jerry Springer show. So we went hog wild with the theater theme to encourage you to get into this divinely engaging story line—to imagine the wreckage of Israel during this period of history and the actual people who were waving their fists in the air and complaining to God about their circumstances. Feel free to give them accents and outfits in your mind, and by all means consider the ways you would fit into this compelling true tale had you been born just a few millennia earlier.

Because this study is discussion-based rather than leader-based, everybody in your group needs to have a chance to share. You don't even have to choose a specific leader for Malachi (which I know can be quite disconcerting for type-A's), because when everyone takes a turn talking about the element of the week's study that most resonated with her, it helps to create a more authentic and inclusive experience. Of course, if you're more comfortable having one friend facilitate the discussion time to keep everybody on track, that's fine. The key is to make this a Bible study discussion group—not a monologue or preaching practice!

Now may I encourage you to exhale before you turn to the next page? Then feel free to doodle in the margins. Be honest. Very few of the questions have right or wrong answers. Throw the book across the room when something I've written steps on one of your emotional bruises or hold it close to your chest when God whispers how much He loves you through a story. My hope is that this parchment-colored tome with a heart on the front cover will become so dear to you that it's soon a familiar fixture on your nightstand or in the passenger seat of your minivan.

Finally, please know that it is an absolute joy and a privilege to stumble toward our Savior with you this season!

Warmly,

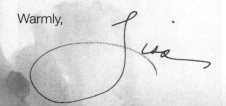

1. when your tarp's trashed (and your dog is dead)

July 4, 2004, was a very bad day. I had just experienced a breakup in a serious dating relationship, so I went over to my friend Kim's house to help her with some household projects and take my mind off my romantic disaster. However, when I was in her garage installing shelves, the ladder I was perched precariously on slipped and crashed, taking me with it to the unyielding cement floor 12 feet below.

I knocked myself out for a few seconds and, when I came to, immediately began interviewing myself mentally: "Can I move my arms and legs?" Yes. "Do I have any bones poking through skin?" No. "Am I bleeding?" Yes. "Am I bleeding a lot?" Yes. "Is anything beginning to swell?" Yes. "Am I thinking clearly?" Sort of.

About that time, Kim came flying around the corner because—as she explained it later—she heard a sound like a big watermelon being split open in the garage. Unfortunately, Kim isn't the calmest person I know at the sight of blood. But after just a few minutes of high anxiety she settled down and began firing her own steady stream of questions: "What's your full name?" "Lisa Dianne Harper." "What's today's date?" "July 4th, 2004." "Who's the president?" "George W. Bush … who I think is quite handsome, by the way."

In spite of what I thought was admirable clarity on my part, Kim wasn't convinced I was OK and insisted on driving me to the nearest hospital. I, on the other hand, was convinced that I was just a bit banged up and didn't want to spend half the night in an emergency room that would inevitably be overcrowded with drunk rednecks who'd barbecued their fingers with fireworks (I love living in Tennessee, but we do have a few rowdy residents). I reasoned that even if I had broken a bone, my doctor could set it the next morning and, in the meantime, I just needed some ice and ibuprofen.

She reluctantly took me inside and began helping me clean up the gashes on my ankle and scalp and made me put frozen peas on the goose egg that had suddenly appeared on my forehead. After a few minutes of being poked and prodded, I remembered that my little Welsh terrier, Reba. (I know it's an unfortunate dog name; she was named by a country songwriter who'd written for Reba McEntire!) Reba was still tied to the picket fence next to the garage, so I asked Kim to go outside and get her.

Kim came back in with a dazed look on her face, announced "Reba's dead," and started laughing. I was pretty discombobulated and assumed Kim was making a terrible joke, so I replied groggily, "That's not funny." To which she stopped laughing. I realized later it was a panicked giggle because my poor friend had more than she could take by that point. Finding me sprawled out on the floor of her garage covered in blood and then discovering Reba in the first stages of rigor mortis had simply done her in.

Then Kim said through tears, "I'm not kidding, Lisa. Reba really is dead."

Evidently my wee red dog had gotten scared by the noise of some prenighttime fireworks someone set off in the neighborhood, and she got tangled up in her leash and hung herself.

To top the whole horrible episode off, after Kim took Reba to the vet to be cremated the next morning (because she felt sorry for me and didn't want me to have to experience anymore grief for awhile), she had a hair appointment with Victor—the guy who gave me Reba. Victor and his wife, Christy, had her for five years before giving her to me when they found out their twins were allergic to dog hair. It had broken Victor's heart to give her up because he loves dogs.

Kim broke the news to him gently soon after sitting down to have her hair cut. Of course, he teared up, then he told her he'd had sinus surgery recently and couldn't blow his nose. After which he tilted his head back and excused himself from the styling area of the salon. He eventually returned but had several more tilting/leaving moments during Kim's haircut. When I saw her again that afternoon, she looked like she'd lost a fight with a weed eater.

In one fell swoop I'd lost my boyfriend, my dog, and a chunk of my head, plus my friend had lost a very cute coiffure. I felt like I had a big sign on my back that read, "Kick me." Have you ever had a season like that, when you felt like everything that could go wrong did go wrong? If so, the good news is you are not alone. Both Scarlett O'Hara and I have been there. I'm pretty sure that's what the Israelites were feeling too … until Malachi picked up a megaphone and began to preach.

Deuteronomy and Malachi are the only books in the Old Testament that begin with a sort of "megaphone address" to all of Israel. In addition, both books emphasize giving generously to God and the blessing that follows a generous heart (see Mal. 3:6–12; Deut. 26:1–19).

video notes:

_____

_____

_____

_____

_____

_____

_____

_____

_____

_____

The Bible is a love story.

rhetorical disputation:
when God's people fuss with God

1. If your group doesn't know one another, introduce yourselves and share what you hope to gain from this study of the Book of Malachi.

2. Did you grow up thinking about the Bible as a textbook, as a book of moral lessons, or as a love story? Describe why.

3. Describe a recent time you felt like Scarlett, fist to the heavens.

"God had written, not so much a poem, but rather a play; a play he had planned as perfect, but which had necessarily been left to human actors and stage-managers, who had since made a great mess of it."

— G.K. CHESTERTON

G.K. Chesterton, *Orthodoxy* (San Francisco: Ignatius Press, 1995), 84.

Video downloads and additional leader helps available at lifeway.com/lisaharper

the historical context

the cast & characters

the literary style

how does Malachi's story
relate to our story?

where does the message of Malachi
challenge our personal stories?

in what ways can I personally
relate to the people of Malachi's day?

THE HISTORICAL CONTEXT

If I heard my dad say this once, I heard it a thousand times: "The fat lady is about to sing." He usually said it while patting his stomach when mom began clearing the dishes at the end of dinner. Or he said it with a grin when the credits begin to roll on his favorite sitcom *All in the Family.* He proclaimed it with a heavy sigh when we loaded the car for the drive back home at the end of a too-short vacation.

Of course, I didn't know "The fat lady is about to sing" was just a colorful colloquialism for the end of something. Therefore I wasted long portions of childhood gaping at heavyset women, half-hoping and half-horrified they were about to burst into uncontrollable warbling.

While not often used in theological settings, I think Dad's politically-incorrect phrase sums up the situation in Malachi. This prophetic book is the exclamation point signaling the end of the Old Testament era, which makes Malachi one of the most significant finales in history—surely enough to make a proverbially pudgy lady want to sing.

what's really going on in Malachi's story?

What's your most recent finale? It might be your child or grandchild's graduation, a retirement party, or the end of some responsibility in church.

What kind of emotion did that particular ending stir up in you?

Malachi is the last book of the Old Testament as it appears in our Bibles. It marks the end of the "Old Revelation" and the beginning of more than four hundred years when God's voice wasn't recorded, aptly called the "Silent Years" or, more formally, "The Intertestamental Period." Therefore, Malachi is essentially God's last speech before the New Testament—the divine drum roll preceding the coming of Jesus Christ.

If you got to create a one-line announcement to accompany the divine drum roll preceding Jesus, what would it be?

How does the Old Revelation differ from divine revelations in the New Testament according to Hebrews 1:1-4?

Despite the climactic placement, biblical historians don't know the exact date for Malachi because neither Scripture nor any writing from antiquity records it. However, we can find some clues to the date. Malachi assumes the second temple in chapters 2–3, and he addresses many of the same issues as Ezra and Nehemiah; marriages to pagans, social injustice, anemic worship, corruption of the priesthood, and so forth. So most scholars place the writing sometime between 460–430 B.C.

Take a few minutes to study the chart on the following page. It sets the stage for Malachi and places his message in context with the Minor Prophets.

The last 12 books of the Old Testament are classified as the Minor Prophets. However this classification has nothing to do with the ancient writers' stature; they weren't necessarily petite men. Their prophecies were simply classified as minor because their books were shorter than those of their more long-winded contemporaries like Isaiah or Jeremiah.

Understanding the setting of Malachi gives our *Gone With the Wind* movie metaphor credence because that's the time period when a group of God's people returned home with Ezra after the captivity in Babylon only to find the land of milk and honey had become an absolute mess. Like Scarlett's beloved Tara, their jewel—the city of Jerusalem—had been trashed.

The Minor Prophets

The first nine books of the Minor Prophets—Hosea, Joel, Amos, Obadiah, Jonah, Micah, Nahum, Habakkuk, and Zephaniah—are usually classified as preexilic, which means they were written prior to that very dark period in Israel's history when Southern Jews were exiled from their homeland and forced to live in captivity in Babylon. The last three books of the Minor Prophets—Haggai, Zechariah, and Malachi—are postexilic, which means these prophets preached after the Jewish exiles returned home to Jerusalem from captivity in Babylon.

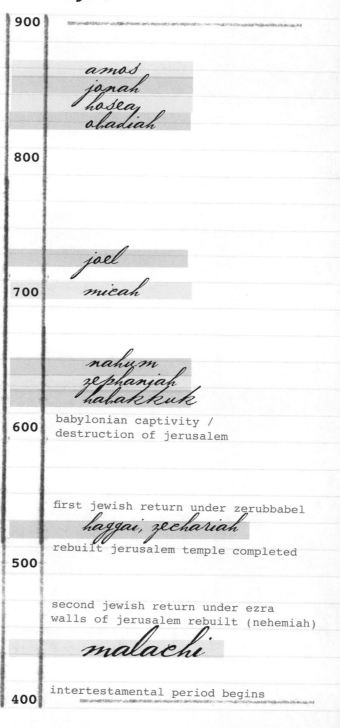

900

amos
jonah
hosea
obadiah

800

joel

700 *micah*

nahum
zephaniah
habakkuk

600 babylonian captivity / destruction of jerusalem

first jewish return under zerubbabel
haggai, zechariah
rebuilt jerusalem temple completed

500

second jewish return under ezra
walls of jerusalem rebuilt (nehemiah)
malachi

400 intertestamental period begins

Can you relate to feeling your Tara has been trashed? If so, describe a season when something (or someone) precious to you was tarnished or destroyed.

How did you respond initially?

One of the effects of disappointment and loss can be exhaustion, which often leads to lethargy. The Israelites display a similar sort of spiritual lethargy in Malachi as we see in Nehemiah. Look through Nehemiah 13:15-31 to answer the following.

What symptoms do you see that indicate spiritual lethargy among the Israelites?

When have you experienced spiritual lethargy, and what were some of your "symptoms"?

THE CAST OF CHARACTERS

Before we explore this culmination tale any further, it behooves us to become familiar with the characters in the story. First there's Malachi, the leading man, whom my dear Italian friend, hairstylist, and former dog-owner, Victor Faragalli, insists should be called *Ma-la-chee.*

In Hebrew the name Malachi literally means "my messenger," implying that Malachi was Yahweh's personal projection system.[1] However, Bible scholars have disagreed through the years about whether Malachi was actually his proper name or his title. Since we have no details about this prophet other than those found in his book, we can't definitively say whether "Malachi" was his name or his job description.

We have no such question about Malachi's vocation as a prophet. Abraham Heschel, a brilliant Jewish scholar, gives us Malachi's detailed job description:

> To the prophets, God was overwhelmingly real and shatter-ingly present. They never spoke of Him as from a distance. They lived as witnesses, struck by the words of God, rather than as explorers engaged in an effort to ascertain the nature of God; their utterances were the unloading of a burden rather than glimpses obtained in the fog of groping.[2]

In that sense, Malachi served as both God's messenger and His megaphone. Can you relate at all to Malachi's experience?

How about you? Would you describe yourself as more of:

a witness, struck by the words of God	an explorer engaged in an effort to ascertain the nature of God

Have you experienced a time when God was "shatteringly present"? If so, what happened and how did you feel?

God's chosen people, the Israelites, make up the second group of characters in this story line. They were handpicked by our Heavenly Father to be His children. They single-handedly de-stroyed the myth that the apple doesn't fall far from the tree, because the Israelites were nothing like their God. They were a motley crew of idolaters and whiners who stumbled into divine grace only because God placed it smack-dab in the middle of their path. Sound familiar?

In light of God's omniscience, why do you think He chose the Israelites to be His ambassadors when He knew full well that they would wobble throughout their walk of faith?

The temple priests form the supporting cast in Malachi's story. These guys were paid to manage God's earthly dwelling place and to give His people spiritual guidance. We're not going to deal with them much until later, but the bottom line is that the Israelites were failing Spirituality 101 largely because their teachers were selfish, lackadaisical buffoons.

THE LITERARY STYLE OF THIS STORY

After returning to their homeland and finding it in ruins, Malachi's peers respond the way spoiled Scarlett did on returning home to a trashed Tara—they raise their fists and fuss. The fancy term for this kind of biblical literary style is *rhetorical disputation,* which basically means that God's people were getting smart with Him.

The rhetorical disputation in Malachi involved four parts:
1. an assertion, followed by
2. questioning,
3. a response, and
4. an implication.

Their first disputation played out like this:

Assertion (from God):

"I have loved you." Malachi 1:2a

Questioning (from Israel/God's people):

"How have you loved us?" Malachi 1:2b

Response(from God):

"Is not Esau Jacob's brother?" declares the LORD.

"Yet I have loved Jacob but Esau I have hated.

I have laid waste his hill country and left his

heritage to jackals of the desert."

Malachi 1:2c-3

Implication (to Israel/God's people):

"Your own eyes shall see this." Malachi 1:5a

Let me make a further clarification about the specific elements of Israel's recorded arguments with God in Malachi.

1. The assertion is a declaration; sometimes God makes it, sometimes Malachi, or sometimes the Israelites make the assertion.
2. The questioning calls the assertion into doubt.
3. The response verifies the assertion because it answers the questioning. When the response comes from God, I like to call it the "big uh-oh" because it captures His comeback to His people's impudence. It reminds me of times I pushed my mom too far when I was a kid and she summoned me by my full name, which usually meant a spanking was in my near future!
4. The implication expresses the consequence of the assertion.

I want to give you a chance to practice identifying the four elements of the rhetorical disputations, so let me send you to one of the shorter examples. The fourth disputation appears in chapters 2–3.

Read Malachi 2:17–3:5 and see if you can identify the four elements. List them by verse reference and by summarizing the statements.

1. the assertion:

2. the questioning:

3. the response:

4. the implication:

HOW DOES MALACHI'S STORY
RELATE TO OUR STORY?

When I taught the Book of Malachi in church recently, I used another movie to underscore the relevance of this minor prophet's story to our own. I showed a clip from *The Scarlet Letter*—the scene where Hester Prynne (who had a brief, passionate love affair with the town's pastor which left her pregnant and unmarried) is forced to wear a red letter "A" around her neck, branding her as an adulteress.

When the clip ended, I pulled out a box filled with lots of big, red letters on lanyards. I solemnly told the class what each letter stood for: *S* represented *sexual sin; P* represented *pride; U* represented *unforgiveness; H* represented *hypocrisy; and I* represented *idolatry.* After explaining what the letters stood for, I hung one of each from my neck. Then I just stood there quietly for a minute.

Which of those five letter(s) accurately represents current sin you're having a difficult time overcoming? You may use your own code since this is for your eyes only.

Within seconds, women began to shift uncomfortably in their seats, assuming I was going to ask them to come to the front of the room and pick pertinent letters out of the box to wear around their necks too. However, I didn't do that because I don't think shame should be welcome in church.

My revealing jewelry did, however, prompt some very interesting and honest conversation about how differently we'd behave if we had our transgressions hanging around our necks like Hester. We probably wouldn't turn up our noses at other sinners, pretending that our wrongdoings were somehow less rotten. We wouldn't be so quick to forget our tendency to wander away from God like the Israelites or whine like Scarlett. And how, if we had to "wear" our sin where everyone could see it, we wouldn't need to be reminded of our desperate need for God's mercy.

According to Lamentations 3:22-23, what keeps us from perishing?

Describe the last time you recognized that you were really desperate for fresh mercy.

How did God deliver His mercy to you? In what specific way did His "new love" affect your heart and mind?

We aren't much different—certainly not any more faithful—than Malachi's buddies. We're headstrong, limping, remedial God-followers too. Thankfully, just as He did with our forefathers long ago, God loves us way too much to leave us mired in our own mistakes with our stubborn fists stuck foolishly in the air.

WHERE DOES THE MESSAGE OF MALACHI CHALLENGE OUR PERSONAL STORIES?

I've had the privilege of touring with Women of Faith for three years now, so most fall weekends I can be found sitting between Sheila Walsh and Natalie Grant. Our seating arrangement tickles me because Sheila and Nat are both award-winning vocalists—they've got enough accolades between them to sink a cruise ship—and I can't carry a tune in a bucket. I'm not being humble; sometimes when I sing it really does sound like someone's choking a cat. Yet as best I understand Scripture on the subject of musical worship, you don't get a pass even if you're tone-deaf, so I obediently belt out every song with gusto.

You know what's amazing? Neither Sheila nor Natalie have ever looked at me sideways when I'm warbling off-key. They've never shushed me or put one finger discreetly in their ears. Although they have more melodic talent in their elbows than I have in my whole body, they let my ugly duckling voice be a part of their beautiful swan choir!

Which reminds me of what I think is the biggest miracle of all in the Book of Malachi—that God let His people fuss. When they had the audacity to question Him for not giving them exactly what they wanted when they wanted it, He could've fried those Israelites into grease spots. He could've zapped their petulant selves into dust bunnies and created a whole new people group who were sweeter and more obedient. But He didn't. Instead our Redeemer let them argue with Him.

He still lets us argue with Him. He gently lowers our white-knuckled fists with His nail-scarred hands. Then, like God's children before us, we stop fussing when we see the compassion in our Father's eyes.

Because God wants us to get the love thing, Scripture is filled with examples. In Judges 6 God had already told Gideon what to do but he repeatedly asked for miraculous confirmation. See Judges 6:36-40.

Why do you think the Creator of the Universe let this wimpy warrior Gideon tell Him to perform a miracle before Gideon would trust Him?

Describe a situation when you told (or were tempted to tell) God to do something before you could trust Him.

Do you think asking God questions and doubting God's merciful sovereignty are synonymous? Why or why not?

When do you think it's permissible to question God?

What are you questioning Him about, honestly through prayer or secretly in your mind and heart, the most about right now?

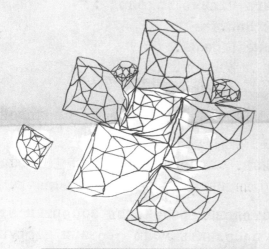

MINING PERSONAL JEWELS FROM MALACHI'S STORY

I'm a firm believer that God infused women with estrogen for a reason. He was being intentional when He wired us to be emotive and sensory-oriented. Therefore, I think God is pleased when we create personal "ebenezers" to commemorate something He's teaching us.

Ebenezer literally means "stone of help."[3] In the Old Testament such stone markers were tangible symbols of God's miraculous provision. In 1 Samuel 7:12-13 Samuel placed an ebenezer on the battlefield to memorialize the victory God gave them over the Philistines. Plus, making ebenezers counts as a craft activity and most women I know become giddy at the mere mention of a glue gun!

So here's how to make the ebenezer for week 1—a tangible reminder of what God is teaching us through Malachi.

Ebenezer

1. Nominate someone cheerful to pick up enough helium balloons for everyone in your small group (with a few extras to account for the popage factor) and bring them to Bible study. Keep in mind that helium balloons are typically free at several chain grocery stores, although the cheerful person might want to drag a child or two along as props.

2. Next, ask everyone in your small group to write the question(s) they'd like to ask God—maybe even fuss with Him about—on a small sheet of paper. When they're finished, have them roll up the question(s) into a small scroll and secure it with a rubber band. Then give everyone a balloon and have them tie their "question scroll" at the end of their balloon's ribbon.

3. Walk outside as a group (or feel free to perform this "trust ritual" individually) and release the balloons.

4. After watching your questions wing their way toward God—or perhaps a power line, which is still under His dominion—compare the reality of Isaiah 55:8-9 with God's redemptive promise in Isaiah 49:11 and then summarize this scriptural amalgamation into your personal prayer* for the week:

Thank you so much for choosing to wobble toward God alongside me through this study of Malachi.

MY HOPE AND PRAYER IS THAT AS A RESULT OF OUR TIME TOGETHER, YOU'LL BECOME MORE CONVINCED THAN EVER BEFORE THAT OUR CREATOR REDEEMER IS SOVEREIGN, MERCIFUL, AND ABSOLUTELY ENAMORED WITH YOU!

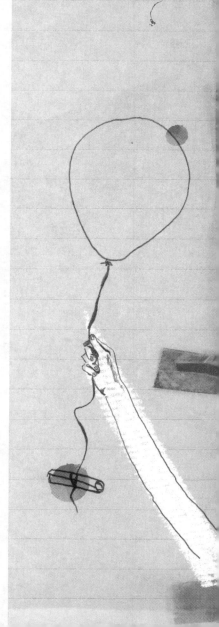

* I'm a big fan of writing memory verses and prayers on index cards and placing them on the bathroom mirror. I've found it helps me stay focused on God's goodness instead of what gravity is doing to my body.

2. God's definitive declaration of affection

I volunteer at a halfway house in downtown Nashville called "The Next Door" that's a faith-based, six-month residential program for women recovering from addiction to drugs or alcohol. If you've ever had the privilege of spending time with recovering addicts you know it's an amazing experience as well as a raggedly honest one. Women who've been busted and spent years in prison as a result don't usually feel the need to wear façades anymore. Frankly, I wish our congregations, small groups, and Sunday school classes were as authentic as my friends are who live in The Next Door house, because I think we're all addicts at heart.

In his book, *Addictions: A Banquet in the Grave,* academic and theologian Dr. Ed Welch wrote: "Addictions are ultimately a disorder of worship."[1] That means we're exhibiting addictive behavior anytime we don't have God squarely in our "soul hole" and so seek to satiate our need for love with anything—or anyone—else. I've never been dependant on drugs or alcohol but I've definitely been addicted to carbohydrates and abusive men.

Well anyway, as a result of volunteering at The Next Door, I've also started going to some Alcoholics Anonymous and Narcotics Anonymous meetings with my friends in recovery. I heard a story recently at one of those meetings that wedged itself deeply into my heart like a redemptive splinter. As is customary at every AA or NA meeting, a woman I'll call Shenequa (not her real name) began with the phrase, "Hi, my name is Shenequa, and I'm an alcoholic-addict." After the rest of the group responded with a hearty, "Hi, Shenequa," she exclaimed with a wide grin, "I was so thankful to be cleaning them tubs today, y'all!" As the rest of her story spilled out, I found out the day of the meeting coincided with her first day of employment at a downtown Nashville hotel.

Shenequa enthused about her new position as a full-time maid because she'd pounded the pavement for over a month and had turned in 114 job applications before finally landing this gig. Mind you, it wasn't her first day of *work* but it was her first eight-hour shift with a company that pays Social Security taxes and gives its employees benefits. Her former job had been selling her body to men who sometimes handed her a $20 bill or a small rock of crack cocaine and often gave her a sexually transmitted disease or a closed fist across the face.

As I listened to Shenequa chatter about how grateful she is to work in a clean, air-conditioned environment with nice people, I found myself wondering how many "tricks" she forced herself to perform to feed her eight young children before committing herself to recovery. How many times she closed her eyes and peeled off her clothes in a desperate attempt to get just one more hit of a narcotic powerful enough to numb her heart and mind to the harsh realities of her life for a few hours.

I can't imagine the torture of dragging myself out of bed every day and trudging through a life that difficult with so little light at the end of the tunnel. Yet not only did Shenequa drag herself out of bed, by the grace of a God she'd heard about as a child and never stopped believing in, she ultimately dragged herself to a treatment center and admitted she needed help defeating the beast of drug addiction.

I don't think I'll ever forget the last thing Shenequa said at that meeting. She explained how she'd stood up to stretch in the hotel bathroom she was cleaning and caught her reflection in the mirror. Her voice caught for a second as she was describing the scene and she took a deep breath to steady herself, then she said softly, "That's the first time since I was a little girl that I looked in the mirror and liked what I seen." Shenequa is beginning to remember who God created her to be. She's beginning to believe again how much her Heavenly Father adores her.

Malachi's peers were polar opposites of Shenequa. Instead of remembering they were God's children who He had always protected and provided for, they were allowing their present-day circumstances to fog up the mirror reflecting their Heavenly

Father's faithfulness. They'd allowed their entire history as recipients of God's lavish mercy to become clouded over. Instead of looking in the glass and smiling in recognition that they bore their divine Dad's image, they focused in on a smudge at the edge and the mildew on the shower curtain behind them. They'd all but forgotten how their value, hope, peace, and future were linked to God's love. So their Creator Redeemer clears His throat, cups His hands around His mouth, and reminds them.

A phrase like "their Creator Redeemer clears His throat, cups His hands around His mouth, and reminds them" is an anthropomorphism, which means attributing human characteristics or behavior to nonhuman things like God or cartoon animals. Anthropomorphisms are often found in biblical imagery, such as when David talks about the heavens being the work of God's "fingers" in Psalm 8:3 to emphasize how even the magnitude of creation is dwarfed by the majesty of our divine King.

video notes:

_____
_____
_____
_____
_____
_____
_____
_____
_____
_____

God has a long history of adoring bumblers like us.

1. When did you first realize God loves girls who limp?

2. How have you sensed God's affection while limping?

3. In your study this week, what did you discover that will help you limp a little less?

"God loves us: not because we are lovable but because He is love, not because He needs to receive but because He delights to give."

— C.S. LEWIS

Walter Hooper, ed., *The Collected Letters of C.S. Lewis*, vol. 3, *Narnia, Cambridge, and Joy 1950–1963* (New York: HarperCollins, 2007), 1951.

Video downloads and additional leader helps available at lifeway.com/lisaharper

scene 1
assertion (from God): Malachi 1:2a

scene 2
questioning (from Israel): Malachi 1:2b

scene 3
response (from God): Malachi 1:2c-3

scene 4
implication (to Israel): Malachi 1:4-5

how often do I truly take God at His word?

SETTING THE STAGE

Yesterday I went for a long trail run in the beautiful Natchez Trace wilderness near where I live in the boondocks south of Nashville. I began my workout with a smile and a happy heart, absolutely smitten by the colors of fall in the canopy of leaves overhead. But halfway up the first big hill, my body began to boycott.

My lower back huffed, "I'm tired of supporting Lisa while she pretends to be a mountain goat; I'm too old for this and have decided to resign." My ankles indignantly replied, "You don't have anything to whine about you big baby, we're the ones stuck down here next to rocks, logs, and horse manure—if she scrapes us again, we're going to pay her back with a nasty sprain." My inner thighs immediately yelled, "Shut up down there! We've got an emergency situation up here. If she runs any faster the friction between us is bound to set this forest on fire!"

My body is in a transitional phase. Swiftly approaching 50, this jar of clay is transitioning from loose to stiff, from resilient to brittle, from perky to saggy. The good news is these physical shifts provide tangible reminders that the earthly existence our Creator allows us is in a constant state of change. I'm learning that the harder we resist change, the harder reality feels when we collide into it headfirst! *Change is inevitable, but trusting God through it is a choice.* The Israelites were in a massive transitional phase during the season Malachi prophesied.

They'd moved from captivity in Babylon back to a degree of independence in Israel; from a secure—albeit confined—existence to risky freedom pockmarked with uncertainty about where they'd live, how they'd put food on the table, and what they should do to protect themselves from their enemies.

What is the biggest transition you're going through right now? Do you feel like you're moving from captivity to freedom, or does your transition seem to be leading you to a more confining place?

The temple their grandparents reminisced about during those long decades in captivity had been demolished. Now standing in its place atop a high hill in Jerusalem was a much smaller church with warped vinyl siding, secondhand furniture, and no big screens for PowerPoint® (see Ezra 3:12).

Does a spiritual "mountaintop" experience in your past cause you to feel nostalgic? If so, do you think it ever keeps you from fully engaging in what God is *currently* doing in your life?

They no longer had the privilege of joyfully serving under a great, divinely chosen king like David and instead had to submit to the authority of a mundane civil ruler (see Mal. 1:8).

Who are some of your favorite former "spiritual leaders" (for example: pastors, Sunday School teachers, or camp counselors from your childhood or adolescence)? Why did they have such a positive impact on you?

Their formerly safe neighborhoods, once filled with the familiar faces of extended family and friends, had morphed into strange, multinational melting pots. Main Street was now dotted with ethnic restaurants. Falafels and pomegranate juice were swiftly being replaced by oblong sandwiches called *burr-eetoes* and fizzy brown drinks called *soe-duhs.* Much to their parent's chagrin, some of their cousins had even married foreigners who talked funny (see Mal. 2:11). Since they didn't like the changes that had come their way, God's people decided to stage a boycott.

Instead of trusting their Heavenly Father—who had *always* provided for them and protected them—they sat down with a collective harrumph, poked out their bottom lips, and began to seriously doubt His goodness.

Can you personally relate to how the Israelites seem to be somewhat stuck in their *past* and dissatisfied with their *present?* If so, in what specific ways can you relate?

INTRODUCING NEW CHARACTERS

We've already met Malachi and his peers, and the Creator Redeemer of the Universe certainly needs no introduction, so the only character left to account for in this disputation is that scaly, scorched-breath, divine antagonist named *Lucifer* (see Isa. 14:12), also known as "Satan" (Job 1:5-7); the Devil (see Matt. 4:1-3); the "dragon" (Rev. 12); the Deceiver (see John 8:42-44); and the "Serpent" or snake (Gen. 3). He's been spewing treachery and deceit since his whopping ego became too heavy for his angelic wings to tote around and he tumbled from God's glorious presence with a resounding splat (see Isa. 14:12-18; Ezekiel 28:12-18; Luke 10:18).

Satan not only lost his ability to fly, he lost his job directing the choir in Heaven and became the chief rival of his former Boss, the Holy Trinity. Since his humiliating plummet from grace, Satan now spends most of his time slinking around here on earth, whispering insidious things into the ears of God's most overwhelmed and exhausted image-bearers.

How has Lucifer tried to lure you away from the promise of God's love lately? (See John 8:42-44.)

The Deceiver has been trying to convince humanity that God didn't—or couldn't—love them since the beginning of time. Remember the hateful stunt he pulled on our great-great and then some grandmother Eve? Here she was completely flabbergasted about being the first female in the universe—I can't begin to imagine the pressure coming with that distinction—and was surely a bit blinded by the sights and sounds of Eden, when the old Snake slithered up next to her and said coyly, "You know *Eva-licious,* if God *really* loved you, He would let you eat the fruit from *any* tree in the garden. I mean you *are* burning the candle at both ends, what with alphabetizing all those names Adam came up with for every creature plus having to carry around all the heavy stuff until the stitches heal from his rib-removal surgery. So I think you deserve to eat whatever you want. If I was your *daddy,* I wouldn't put *any* restrictions on you!"

Ugh, makes you want to rip that forked tongue right out of his mouth, doesn't it? Unfortunately, in Malachi's day the nation of Israel was in such a state of disappointment and despair regarding the changes they faced on returning home from Babylon that they stopped standing guard against the lizard bent on their destruction. Soon enough the lies he was whispering about God's lack of affection and concern for them began to sound uncannily like the truth. Let's look at the first disputation.

Israel is the only nation ever specifically chosen by God for a covenantal relationship. The Old Testament historical books—Joshua, Judges, Ruth, 1 Samuel, 2 Samuel, 1 Kings, 2 Kings, 1 Chronicles, 2 Chronicles, Ezra, Nehemiah, and Esther—reveal how God established Israel as His very own people group and how He chose the Israelites to be His ambassadors to other nations.

scene one

ASSERTION (FROM GOD):

"I have loved you," says the LORD.

Malachi 1:2a

In rhetorical disputation what God says *first* typically sets the tone and creates the "flavor" for the whole passage. This means the first prophetic meal served in Malachi began with dessert because it just doesn't get any sweeter than the Creator of the Universe saying *I. Have. Loved. You.*

The tense of the Hebrew verb in Malachi 1:2a could be translated with the phrase, " 'I love you,' Yahweh said."[2] In this simple statement, God clarifies that He has *already* fulfilled the deepest desire of every human heart to be fully known, completely accepted, and unconditionally adored. God wasn't holding up a carrot trying to tempt the Israelites back toward faithfulness. He's not saying, "If y'all straighten up and behave like I told you, then I'll think about loving you." There's no condition to God's pronouncement of enduring affection. It's not a wobbly, if-the-planets-align-I'll-do-it, kind of pledge. It's a statement of historical fact. The Creator of the Universe had loved His chosen people, the Israelites, throughout every single moment of their lives.

How does your head react to the fact that God loves you?

How about your heart? What emotional response does the fact of God's affection for you prompt?

I think the way our Heavenly Father communicates His compassion without guile is the *bomb!* I'm so glad God isn't a coy suitor. He doesn't act like a seventh-grade boy at the movies with us who jams His hands in His pockets in an attempt to look cool. Thank goodness the Lover of our soul has instead always been publicly passionate about His people. Remember how He advertised His relationship with the Israelites in the wilderness? How He hovered over them like a cloud by day and a pillar of fire at night (see Ex. 13:17-22)? That's like a supernatural blimp of commitment—God's overt declarations of affection make Barry White sound like a lisping schoolboy. Anybody blushing yet?

Read Song of Songs 2:4; 4:9. What's the most overt romantic gesture someone's ever done for you? How did you react to their overture?

Humanly speaking, whose affection (romantic, platonic, or familial) can you trust in the most? When you look back over the course of your life, has someone *always* seemed to love you? If so, who is that person (or people) and why do you think their love for you is so consistent?

When have you felt the most secure in God's everlasting love for you? (See Ps. 136:2; Rom. 8:35-39.)

On a scale of 1 to 10, with 1 being *absolute disbelief* and 10 being *absolute security,* how confident are you regarding God's affection for you today?

absolute
disbelief

absolute
security

scene two

QUESTIONING (FROM ISRAEL):

"How have you loved us?" Malachi 1:2b

In spite of God's ardency, Malachi's buddies arched their eyebrows in doubt over His assertion. After a slow, sweeping look at the poverty and chaos surrounding them, they let out a long sigh and asked, *"How* have you loved us?"

The first time I studied the Book of Malachi and read their cheeky inquiry, I was tempted to retort, "Really, y'all? I mean, come on! Yahweh rescued you from Egypt, He dried up an entire ocean so you wouldn't get your tootsies wet on your trek to freedom, He showered you with Twinkies in the wilderness, and He gave you first dibs on national holidays—*Come on!* How about a little less whining here, people? How about showing some gratitude instead of calling God's fidelity into question?"

When I silenced the peanut gallery in my head and really pondered the starkness of the Israelite's postexilic circumstances—how they'd attended one too many funerals of their friends and family members, how their national dignity had been dragged through the mud, how they'd been forced to drain their savings accounts and rack up huge debt just to eek out a living, and how they lugged boxes of their meager possessions downstairs to their mother-in-law's tiny basement to have someplace indoors for their kids to sleep—I stopped judging and started empathizing.

Because I know what it's like to become so distracted by my own disappointment, so preoccupied with my own pain, that I glance right past God's grace. I'm not minimizing the fact that the Israelites doubted God's mercy, but I can totally relate to it. I'm guilty of wasting big chunks on the calendar of my life living like an emotional agnostic too. How about you?

Compare God's covenant promises to Abraham (founding father of the Israelite nation) with what actually occurred prior to Malachi's era by reading Genesis 12:1-3; 2 Chronicles 36:15-23.

In light of their recent history, how much hope do you think the Israelites held out that God would actually come through on what He had promised Abraham?

What "hope deferred" (an unfulfilled dream or promise, Prov. 13:12) made you the most heartsick in the past?

With what unfulfilled dream are you currently dealing?

Has your disappointment made you move toward God or away from Him? Why do you think it has that effect?

A holy song is a wonderful illustration of how God *allows* His people to wrestle honestly with disappointment. The psalms were originally crafted as the hymn book of the Old Testament.[3] Read Psalm 42 and ask yourself how would you relate this divine blues tune to the seasons of your life thus far?

How would you relate in the beginning (vv. 1-4)?

How would you relate in the middle (vv. 5-7)?

How would you relate in the end (vv. 8-11)?

scene three

RESPONSE (FROM GOD):

"Is not Esau Jacob's brother?" declares the LORD. "Yet I have loved Jacob but Esau I have hated. I have laid waste his hill country and left his heritage to jackals of the desert." Malachi 1:2c-3

God's response here seems odd if not completely disconnected, as if He got distracted by a football game playing on the television behind Israel's head and forgot what they were talking about for a moment. But of course, that can't be the case because our Creator is perfectly omniscient and never misses a beat. God has simply switched gears in their conversation to jar the Israelites into considering the historicity of His faithfulness.

I can totally picture them leaning forward when God asked the rhetorical question: "Is not Esau Jacob's brother?" Because they realized immediately that He was referring to a colorful story about two brothers—fraternal twins actually—named Jacob and Esau who got themselves into the messiest food fight of all times. The Israelites were familiar with this tale because it had been told and retold among them for generations.

The story began with Abraham and Isaac. When Isaac was 40 years old he married Rebekah, but they had no children. Isaac prayed for Rebekah, and God answered his prayer. Rebekah became pregnant, but it was a troubled pregnancy with twins who fought in her womb. She went to God to ask about the struggle within her, and God told her she was bearing two nations. The boys born to her would sire two countries and the older would serve the younger.

In the ancient Near Eastern language of Malachi, the antonyms love and hate are not indicative of petty human emotion. In fact, the biblical idiom "to hate" usually means to love someone or something less rather than to have extreme animosity for someone or something (see Gen. 29:30-33; 1 Sam. 1:2-5; Matt. 10:37; Luke 14:25-26).

Isaac was 60 years old when the boys were born. The first was reddish and hairy; they named him Esau meaning *Hairy.* The other brother was born with his fist clutched tight to Esau's heel; they named him Jacob, meaning *Heel.*

When the boys grew up, Esau became an outdoorsman and a hunter. Jacob became a quiet man preferring life indoors. Isaac loved Esau because he loved to eat the game Esau brought home, but Rebekah loved Jacob.

One day Jacob was cooking a stew. Esau came in from the field, starved. Esau said to Jacob, "Give me some of that red stew—I'm starved!" That's how he came to be called Edom (Red). Jacob said, "Make me a trade: my stew for your rights as the firstborn." Esau said, "I'm starving! What good is a birthright if I'm dead?" Jacob said, "First, swear to me." And he did it. On oath Esau traded away his rights as the firstborn. Jacob gave him bread and the stew of lentils. He ate and drank, got up and left. That's how Esau shrugged off his rights as the firstborn.
Genesis 25:29-34, Message

The kicker of this true tale is that Hairy's (Esau) offspring grew up and formed the nation of Edom, while Heely's (Jacob) offspring went on to become the nation of Israel. Largely because of how Esau squandered his inheritance on a bowl of chili, God chose Jacob—the younger twin—to be the specific grandson of Abraham through whom His covenant people, the Jews, would come. Sadly, all of Esau's kids and grandkids and great-grandkids were sentenced to live their lives outside the circle of God's sovereign favor. Ultimately, as a result of their continued rebellion against God, all the inhabitants of Edom were completely destroyed.

My guess is the Israelite's eyes got really round after this response from God because His words were a thunderous reminder of their status as class favorites.

Reread Genesis 25:19-34 in your Bible. With which of the twins do you identify most? Why?

Do you think it's "fair" that God favored Jacob over Esau? Explain.

How does the story of Jacob and Esau shed light on Paul's sermon in Ephesians 2 about our salvation being a free gift from God that isn't based on our morality or lack thereof?

Isaiah chapters 34–35 describes the future for the descendants of Jacob and Esau. Chapter 34 pictures the future for Edom (see Isa. 34:9-10). Chapter 35 focuses on Israel's future from Isaiah's perspective.

If you were writing a book or a screenplay about either of those chapters, what title would you give each?

Edom's future:

Israel's future:

Which verse from Isaiah 35 would you choose as a theme verse for your and/or your family's future?

How would you paraphrase that theme verse into language that a child could understand?

Read Matthew 10:37; Luke 14:25-27. Who have you had to *love less* to get closer to Jesus?

scene four

IMPLICATION (TO ISRAEL):

"Your own eyes shall see this."

Malachi 1:5

Those of us who speak or sing at Women of Faith conferences get pretty punchy because we have to sit on a side stage for about three hours on Friday night and then All. Day. Long. Saturday. I honestly think my bottom has gotten flatter and wider over the past few years as a result! However, since the cameras often pan in our direction thereby projecting us on giant screens for all the attendees to see, our bosses expect us to behave. But sometimes we just can't help ourselves.

Such was the case recently when seconds before Sheila Walsh walked on-stage I bet her she couldn't weave the word *raccoon* into her talk. Someone had told a story about raccoons raiding their trash cans on our break so it was the first unsuitable word that came to my mind.

Brave Scottish lass that she is, Sheila wasn't even rattled by my last-second dare. Instead she grinned at me triumphantly and said, "Done!" before waltzing onstage. I don't remember exactly how she wove raccoon into her expositional message from the New Testament, but I do remember it was seamless.

The implication here in verse 5 is the divine version of "Done!" It's a definitive promise from the Creator and Sustainer of the Universe that the Israelites will see the permanent demise of their archenemy, the Edomites. Yet in spite of their galvanizing history lesson only moments before, I think Malachi's peers now furrowed their eyebrows and crossed their arms dubiously. Because from their finite human perspective, Edom was still flourishing and they were still floundering. It was as if God had prematurely presented the Oscar to a clumsy ingénue who'd forgotten her lines *and* fallen off the stage while Meryl Streep was waiting in the wings dressed in Armani couture. His "done" just didn't seem plausible given their current circumstances.

The little Book of Obadiah speaks to the nation of Edom. "Though you soar aloft like the eagle, though your nest is set among the stars, from there I will bring you down, declares the LORD" (Obad. 4).

Do you know someone who's currently flying high like an eagle in spite of the fact that they're deceitful, abusive, and/or extremely self-centered? If so, how do you feel about the fact that they seem to be benefitting from hurting others—perhaps even you?

In Psalm 69 David poured out his heart in a time of great distress. Read Psalm 69:16-29 and describe the season in your life when you could most identify with some of David's complaints in this sad song.

Do you typically consider God slow when it comes to judging the wicked people who are polluting your little corner
of the world or just right with regard to how and when He
doles out consequences to the wicked?

Psalm 139:19-24 makes some rather radical statements
about hating the enemies of God. How would you describe
the healthy tension between having a strong heart that
rears up against evil and having a soft heart that submits to
the authority of the Holy Spirit?

Imagine you are teaching Sabbath school in Malachi's time.
How would you explain Romans 5:1-5 to the Israelites?

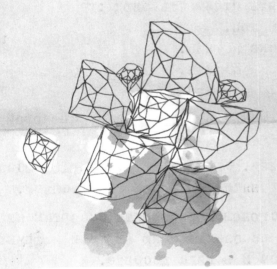

MINING PERSONAL JEWELS FROM MALACHI'S STORY

Write Romans 5:1-5 as nicely and neatly as you can on an index card or sheet of paper with your nondominant hand. If you're right-handed, use your left hand and vice versa; if you're ambidextrous, this is going to be a piece of cake! While you're writing out all five verses, pray for God to help you appreciate things that take a long time. Then when you finish, post your artwork in a public place like your refrigerator at home or your computer monitor at the office to practice appreciating something that took a relatively long time to create and didn't come out perfectly!

Learning to Hope

1. **Create** a top 10 waiting list of things you've almost stopped hoping for.

2. **Pray** through your list, asking God to breathe life into the hopes and dreams that are in alignment with His will for your life and to give you wisdom regarding what hopes and dreams to let go of.

3. **Consider sharing** your waiting list with a few other Christian girlfriends in order to have support in this journey toward really taking God at His word!

3. going big or going home

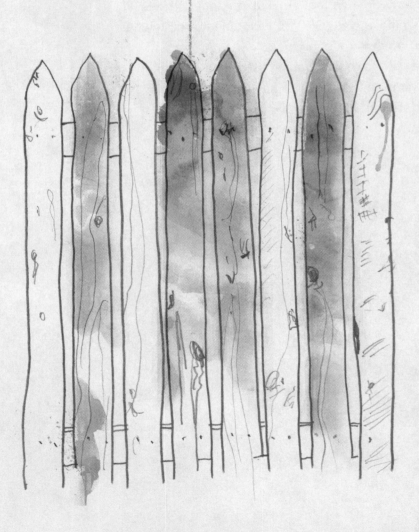

Despite my aging body's protests, I love trail-running. Dirt paths through the woods appeal to me infinitely more than running around a cement oval or a sidewalk. I'd rather hear birds chirping than car horns and squealing breaks. I'd definitely rather glimpse a timid white-tailed deer bounding through the trees than another large man lumbering along in too-short shorts.

Trail-running isn't just a workout to me, it's a wonderful way to unwind. It makes stress evacuate my heart like spraying a garden hose causes my neighbor's pesky cat to sprint away from my roses. What I didn't bargain for is that careening along rocky trails would cause part of my nose to leave my face.

I was happily racing down a path in the Natchez Trace wilderness area, when I hit a slick spot. Instantly I was sprawling through the air. I crash-landed with my arms extended in an instinctive Superman pose. Unfortunately the steep trail and my momentum propelled my head into the ground like a snowplow, causing me to dig a trench with my chin. Even more unfortunately, the trail I was on is strewn with rocks and my face rammed into a sharp one with so much force that it sliced my nose right up the middle.

It took a few seconds to gather my wits after that ungainly face-plant but sobered up quickly when I realized blood was spurting from my nose. I didn't have time to panic or whine because I was in a remote area—several miles from help—so I held my mangled sniffer together with my T-shirt and ran to my car, praying out loud the whole time. A surgeon friend met me at the ER and stitched my snout back together. It's still healing, and the latest prognosis is my nose won't ever look like it used to, but it won't be "hideous" either. The moral of the story is what my friend Paige said when she came to see me at the hospital. "Lisa, when you're teaching about how we should live with passion for the sake of the gospel you're going to have to quit saying, 'We need to leave skin on the table!' "

"Skin on the table" is my paraphrase of Jesus' command about sacrificial living: "Whoever loses his life for my sake will find it" (Matt. 16:25b). When encouraging my friends in addiction recovery, I'd say things like, "Getting sober is going to take all the strength you have and then some. You're going to have to leave some skin on the table, but with Jesus you can win this fight!" When talking with friends at the point of giving up on their marriage, I'd say things like: "God can redeem this. But you're going to have to invest your heart in him again, and it will definitely get dinged up in the process. Are you willing to leave more skin on the table?"

After my close encounter of the nose kind, I've decided to rephrase my own paraphrase. I think perhaps a better way to describe Jesus' call to live sacrificially is "go big or go home."

"Go big or go home" comes naturally to me. I'm a born risk-taker. Mom said I walked at 8 months, ran before my 1st birthday, and haven't slowed down since. Dad Harper encouraged my wild side by buying me my first motorcycle—a darling orange Honda 70—when I was 7 years old. Less than an hour after tearing the red ribbon off, the steel forks were bent and I had a bloody lip. Because I tried to be like Evel Knievel and jump a sinkhole!

I graduated to bigger and faster bikes culminating in a black and silver Harley I bought for my 40th birthday. I've also swum with sharks off Central America, barefoot waterskied, and raced mountain bikes competitively in Colorado. I took up snowboarding in my 30s, and I'm taking hip-hop classes in my 40s. Physically, I think I've always lived a "go big or go home" kind of life.

However, emotionally, my life used to be anything but big because long before I hopped on that little pumpkin-colored rocket, I'd learned to protect my heart. I was 5 when Dad Harper walked away from my mom, my sister, and me and to another woman and her son. Abandonment filleted my heart like that rock filleted my nose … only it hurt worse. I was too little to understand so I thought his departure must be my fault. I thought if only I'd been prettier or sweeter or somehow better Dad wouldn't have left us.

Over the next two years I was molested by several men, who came and went from our fractured family, which poured shame into the aching crevasse that already split my heart in two. Then when my stepfather John turned out *not* to be the loving new daddy I'd prayed so hard for, bricks of disappointment sealed off the wound in my soul. As I grew taller, my fear of intimacy got bigger too. I feared that if I allowed anybody inside the fortress of my heart and they saw how disfigured and messy it was in there, they'd walk away like Dad or hurt me like those other men had. I couldn't stand the thought of being abandoned or abused again.

It took a long time—coupled with Christian counseling, the fervent prayers of dear friends, and countless hours spent soaking my calloused soul in the sweet salve of Scripture—to believe that God not only has my back, He cradles my heart. To believe the same mighty mitts that set the stars in place hold me securely and will never let go. I'm slowly learning to let the Creator of the Universe double as my bodyguard because when I used up my energy trying to protect myself I had none left to engage in great things and great people. My self-protective posture limited me from experiencing the amazing life Jesus purchased for us on Calvary. Now that I'm not trying to hold up that wall around my heart, my hands are free to do all kinds of cool stuff!

My slow-to-gain grasp of "go big or go home" has given me a different take on the second disputation. I used to think Malachi 1:6-14 was all about anemic tithing, the essence of what I'd heard preached. But I've come to believe it's about much more than dinky checks the Israelites put in the offering plate. It's about how they'd stopped believing Yahweh had their backs and cradled their hearts. How in their disbelief, they'd begun hoarding food to ensure that their kids would have enough to eat and hoarding crumpled bills under their mattresses to ensure they could make it on their own in case divine provision failed.

God's people weren't simply being stingy; they weren't giving the Creator His due because their hands were too busy placing orange cones around their crippling national fear and building a fence around the gaping wounds in their psyches. They couldn't "go big or go home" because they'd forgotten what "home" was. They couldn't even remember where to park their hope.

session 3. video & group guide

video notes:

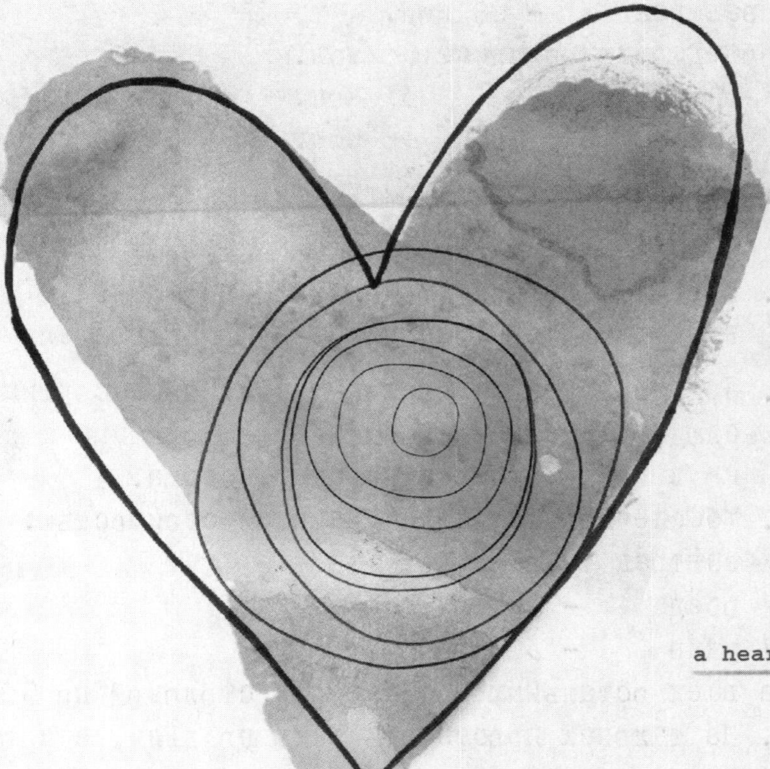

a heart for worship

Jeremiah 2:13

1 Corinthians 6:19-20

kardia

1. Thinking about "going big or going home" with your heart when it comes to God, in what ways to do you need to step out of your box and "go bigger" with God?

2. How does the definition "moving toward Jesus" make you think differently about *worship*?

3. To which broken cistern do you most often run when you're thirsty for attention or affection? How has Christ filled your broken cisterns?

"Worship as adoration of God is a distinctive activity; it embraces both understanding and emotions, the whole person in the presence of the God of creation and redemption. ... Even so, this does not mean turning away from the world. It involves, rather, the right perception of how God relates to the world, and the world to God. In such a framework, worship, embracing both adoration and action, is nothing but the outworking of God-centredness in the individual and corporate experience of the people of God."

—D.A. CARSON

D.A. Carson, ed., *Worship: Adoration and Action* (Eugene, OR: Wipf and Stock Publishers, 2002), 17–18.

scene 1.
assertion (from God) – Malachi 1:6a-c

scene 2.
questioning (from Israel) – Malachi 1:6d

scene 3.
response (from God) – Malachi 1:7a

scene 4.
questioning (from Israel) – Malachi 1:7b

scene 5.
response (from God) – Malachi 1:7c-8a

scene 6.
implication (to Israel) – Malachi 1:6-14

> how has fear made me less generous with
> my affection, time, and money?

SETTING THE STAGE

One of my dear friends (who will remained unnamed for obvious reasons) has a mother-in-law who's the absolute worst gift-giver I've ever met. The first Christmas her son and my friend were married, she gave her brand-new daughter-in-law a single gift: an ornament. Which doesn't sound that bad until you find out the date on the ornament was *3 years old*. On other celebratory occasions she has presented my friend with a macramé toilet paper holder, a not-so-gently-used theme sweater embedded with multiple strands of someone else's hair, an old toaster with only one working slot, and various other tacky knickknacks and broken household appliances.

Before I go any further, I want to clarify that I wouldn't be dogging my friend's mother-in-law if she was financially strapped or vision-impaired. If she couldn't afford to pick up a little present at Target or couldn't see the sort of junk she was trying to pass off as "gifts," I wouldn't have taken offense on behalf of my buddy. But this woman is neither poor—she spends wads of cash on herself and her dogs—nor blurry-eyed—she's quick to point out the faintest spots on their rug and miniscule dust particles on their bookshelves. Which leads me to believe that her cheap gifts are indicative of how little she values her relationship with her daughter-in-law.

Imagine yourself as my friend. How would you feel toward your cheap gift-giving mother-in-law?

Judging from the cheap gifts the priests were hauling into the temple, the Israelites weren't putting much value into their relationship with God either. Disappointment and disbelief had squeezed most of the hope from their lives, and in the same way you can't get much toothpaste out of a tube that's been squished to the bottom end, so too the Jewish priests were down to their last dredges of worship. Instead of handing over the best the Israelites had to offer in adherence to the Torah—which meant sacrificing big bulls, ripe olives, and unblemished lambs—they were keeping the best for themselves and squeezing the leftover skinny cows, bruised fruit, and crippled sheep into the offering plate. Instead of "going big" so as to show God the honor and respect He is due, those in charge of the temple "went tiny," assuming their Boss wouldn't notice. But God noticed all right, and boy did He get ticked!

INTRODUCING NEW CHARACTERS

Although the Israelite priests were briefly introduced in Malachi 1, their intimate involvement in the following scenes necessitates a more detailed description. You probably remember that God established the Israelite priesthood during the time Moses was leading Israel and He decreed that priests had to come directly through the lineage of Moe's brother Aaron (see Ex. 28–29).

Not only did these ancient spiritual leaders have to be natural descendants of Aaron, they had to marry either a virgin or a widow of Jewish descent. The "high priest" only had the option of marrying a Jewish virgin (see Lev. 21:13-15), which meant no e-harmony romantic smorgasbords for these guys. Plus, priests weren't allowed to have any physical defects or deformities (see Lev. 21:16-23), which was a total bummer for the boys in Aaron's family tree who were born with cute strawberry birthmarks or wee webbed toes.

Obviously, God set very high standards for this fraternity of holy men charged with keeping the Israelites on track spiritually. Unfortunately, by the time the postexilic era rolled around those divine standards had been all but forgotten and the holy hierarchy Yahweh created had digressed into a motley crew of less-than-faithful frat boys.

scene one

ASSERTION (FROM GOD):

A son honors his father, and a servant his
   master. If then I am a father, where is
   my honor? And if I am a master, where is
   my fear? says the LORD of hosts to you, O
   priests, who despise my name. Malachi 1:6

Because I live way out in the country, people don't usually visit at night without calling first. We have coyotes, turkeys, opossums, and deer cavorting around out here after dark, but most people choose to avoid that kind of wild animal revelry. However recently an acquaintance came over late at night without calling ahead first and definitely without an invitation.

I was startled when I heard her banging on my front door and even more startled by her anxious expression. I immediately assumed she'd been in a traffic accident on the highway that runs in front of my house because why else would this relative stranger (I'd only met her a few times previously in social settings) show up on my front porch all disheveled and disrupt me from watching Letterman?

When I asked her if I should call 911, she replied, "No, I came out here to talk to you." I quickly realized while she didn't need an ambulance, she might need a therapist. I cautiously invited her into the living room and brought her some water but before I could ask any questions, she launched into a very emotional monologue about how she was considering leaving her husband and four children to be in a lesbian relationship.

When she finally took a breath and paused her love triangle litany, I told her I'd be glad to pray for her because God promises to direct our paths when we ask Him for help. At which point she flipped her hair and asked coyly, "Do you think I'm weird?"

I replied, "I don't know you well enough to have an opinion about whether or not *you're* weird. However I think this *situation,* the fact that you came to my house in the middle of the night when you barely know me and are divulging intimate details about your life and other people's lives, *is* weird."

When she finally calmed down and stopped crying, *"Why* don't you like me?" I prayed for her to have peace, the kind of perfect peace you can only find in Jesus. Then I gave her the name and number of a wonderful Christian counselor and escorted her back to her car.

As I watched her taillights fade away, I felt a wave of resentment rise up in my soul. I didn't like how that chick dumped her bag of problems on the floor of my heart without even asking first. How she wasn't trying to build relationship—those usually begin with casual conversation over a cup of coffee. She just wanted to stick her finger down her throat and vomit up all her bad feelings regardless of how her junk splattered on anyone else.

It's one thing for someone to be self-centered, exploitative, and disrespectful toward you, but it's a whole other thing when they're self-centered, exploitative, and disrespectful toward you in your own home.

Have you experienced someone dumping their trash in your heart, uninvited? If so, what bothers you about such experiences?

That woman's actions parallel what was taking place during Malachi's tenure as Israel's prophet. Most of the priests in God's neighborhood of Jerusalem were behaving less like spiritual leaders and more like mafia middlemen. They set up kiosks on the temple grounds and were advertising scratch-and-dent objects as "perfect offerings." Of course the Israelites bought what they were selling. Those greedy priests might as well have been hawking Graham crackers, marshmallows, and chocolate bars at a bonfire because the Israelites knew they were supposed to purchase a sacrifice—a gift—for Yahweh before walking up the steps to the temple, before entering *His house.*

Most of those regular Joes were probably oblivious to the fact they'd just paid full-price for damaged goods. Or maybe they were just too tired to care, but the priests were laughing all the way to the bank with bags full of dirty money extorted from their crooked "worship" deals.

In Exodus 23:19 and Proverbs 3:9-10 what did God command His people to give as worship offerings?

The firstfruits literally meant the best fruit from the initial harvest of their crops. Since most of us aren't vocational farmers, what do you think the modern application of "giving our firstfruits" to God is?

Do you find it more difficult to give God affection, time, or money? Why do you think one is harder to part with than the other?

The Old Testament word for "heart" is lêb̄ab̄, and rather than referring to the muscle in our chest, it's typically used in reference to the core of our being— to our thought life, emotions, and understanding.[1]

Reread Malachi 1:6. The English word "honor" in this verse is translated from the Hebrew word *k̄āb̄od̄*, which literally means "heavy."[2] Therefore when a son honors his father, he is actually giving him *weight.*

How do you typically honor, or *give weight to,* the people you respect?

scene two

QUESTIONING (FROM ISRAEL):

But you say, "How have we despised your name?" Malachi 1:6d

My little brother, John Price, has such a sweet smelling spirit—he's tenderhearted, easy-going, and generous—but I think he may have the stinkiest feet on the planet! I'll never forgot one night when we were sitting next to each other at a church "youth night" I'd dragged him to. J.P.'s eight years younger than I am and was thus a natural target for my early evangelistic zeal. I smelled a horrible, and I mean *horrible,* odor wafting from him.

I was already a little miffed by J.P.'s adolescent slouch, the way he was picking at his cuticles and his obvious lack of interest in everything the speaker was preaching. Therefore when he rudely "broke wind" in the sanctuary,—my mother lectured us a lot about this particular body function when we were growing up and my friends tease me about how persnickety I still am when the subject comes up—that was my last straw.

The word "name" in verse 6 is translated from the Hebrew word *šēm,* which has a much richer and broader meaning than the English definition. The semantic range for *šēm* includes the concepts of "identity, character, significance, power, authority, presence, essence, representation."[3] Therefore when God accuses the Israelite priests of despising His *name,* the implication is that they have actually rejected and disobeyed *Him.*

I attempted to convey how appalled I was by breathing a heavy, put-upon sigh and shooting a withering glance in his direction. After he completely ignored a whole series of sighs I elbowed him sharply in the ribs.

John turned his head toward me with furrowed brows and mouthed indignantly, "What?"

I pursed my lips like a fussy old librarian and then whispered accusingly through clenched teeth, "That was disgusting and I can't believe you did it in church!"

John raised his hands, palms up, shrugged his shoulders, and whispered, "What in the world are you talking about?"

I whispered back, "You know *exactly* what I'm talking about!"

He slumped down in his seat and muttered, "You're crazy."

I should've left well enough alone. Or at least let the subject drop until the service was over and we were outside. But I just couldn't stand the fact that he wouldn't admit his faux pas. So I pressed the matter and declared a little too loudly, "When we get home I'm going to tell Mom that you *passed gas* in church!"

To which John sat up like a shot and retorted heatedly, and very loudly, *"I did not!"*

Of course by now the good people seated in the pews around us had become acutely aware of our disagreement, as well as what it was about. There were snickers. Some leaned in to hear how I would respond to John's denial.

I won't belabor our silly sibling spat any longer except to say we eventually discovered that the real culprit was John's *shoes*—a pair of leather Top-Siders he insisted on wearing without socks—which had become imbued with the stink of a thousand skunks. To this day when we reminisce about that odiferous evening, J.P. delights in reminding me he was technically innocent!

It's impossible to tell if any members of the priesthood were technically innocent of dishonoring Yahweh's name. Malachi didn't videotape his message so we don't know which, if any, of their voices were sincere when they cried out: "How have we despised your name, Yahweh?"

Maybe some of the younger priests were so far removed from the inner workings of the scratch-and-dent system that they *really* didn't know how corrupt it actually was. Surely some of them were in the same disengaged posture that J.P. adopted on that Tuesday night so long ago—slouched in a temple cubicle, preoccupied with their own thoughts, not really paying attention to the God they were working for. But whether they were intentionally holding back from their Heavenly Father or not, their stench of disrespect still stank to high Heaven.

Read James 4:17. Do you think the consequences for sins of "commission" (when we actually *do something* God said not to do) should be as harsh as the consequences for sins of "omission" (when we *don't do something* God said to do)? Why or why not?

When are you most likely to "slouch" in God's presence?

Where does your mind most often wander during prayer?

What kind of things do you tend to do, or *not* do, when you're in a public worship setting like church in an effort to show God honor and respect (for example, dressing modestly, not "hollering," and so forth)?

Read 1 Corinthians 8:9-13; 9:13-23. How would you describe the difference between *having appropriate respect for God in church/His house* and *following oppressive religious rules* (like only being allowed to read from certain Bible translations or women having to wear hose) so as to appear reverent?

scene three

RESPONSE (FROM GOD):

By offering polluted food upon my altar.

Malachi 1:7a

During a sleepover at my dad's house when I was in middle school, Karen Easton asked me to smoke some cigarettes she'd pilfered from her mom's purse. She assured me we wouldn't get caught because she'd done the same thing several times before with LuAnn Mansfield.

I wasn't too excited about smoking cigarettes—and was afraid I might go to hell if I did—but I really wanted Karen to like me so I gave in and took one of the contraband Virginia Slims she was offering.

I did my best to imitate her long, slow drags for a few minutes and then told her we'd better put them out because Dad was due back from the store any moment. We opened several windows, sprayed my stepmother's perfume liberally around the living room, and flushed all the butts down the toilet in the hall bathroom. Then we hunkered down on the couch, our mouths stuffed full of Dentyne, and commenced playing Atari.

When I heard Dad's car pull into the driveway, droplets of guilt from all over my body coagulated to form a large mass in my stomach. I squeaked nervously, "Oh no, that's him!"

Karen, who was older and therefore wiser in the ancient art of parent-fooling, shushed me and barked, "Be cool!"

I managed a weak smile and a wave when Dad walked in the door. Then exhaled the breath I'd been holding when he said, "Good night girls," and started walking down the hallway toward his bedroom. Thinking we'd gotten away with our crime, Karen flashed me a cat-that-ate-the-canary grin and a thumbs-up sign.

But then we heard Dad's footsteps hesitate outside of the hall bathroom and before we knew it he was marching back toward us with something in hand.

The guilt-tumor in my belly migrated to my throat when Dad reached down and turned off the television before turning his attention toward Karen and me.

When he opened his hand to reveal four soggy cigarette butts, it burst out of my mouth in, "I'm so sorry Dad!" sobs. I could tell Karen was bugged that I caved in so quickly, but what was a preteen defendant to do when her father unveiled the smoking gun (no pun intended)?

What do you think the Israelite priests and the kleptomaniac couple in Acts 4:32–5:10 have in common?

If you got to write a children's book that recounted the tale of Ananias and Sapphira, what title would you give the moral of your story?

In Psalm 51 when David expressed his yearning to be reconciled with God, his was an altogether different response to being found guilty of sin than the way the priests reacted when God pronounced them guilty in Malachi 1:6-14.

Describe a situation when you were convicted of creating distance between yourself and God and responded with genuine repentance like David.

Can you also describe a time when you had less humility and behaved more like the Israelite priests?

scene four

QUESTIONING (FROM ISRAEL):

"How have we polluted you?" Malachi 1:7b

One of my pet peeves is when someone knows beyond a shadow of a doubt they've hurt somebody else yet tries to wriggle out of the mess they made by saying, *"If* I've done anything that hurt you, please forgive me." I much prefer it when people own their mistakes outright. Based on what I've read in the Bible, I think our Redeemer does too.

John 4 contains the famous meeting between Jesus and the woman at the well. When the woman requested living water, Jesus' response "Go, call your husband" (v. 16) revealed she needed to face the facts of her life first. To which she responded with the technically accurate but less-than-transparent statement "I have no husband" (v. 17).

How would you describe Jesus' response to this woman's evasion? (See John 4:17-18.)

Do you find our Redeemer's bluntness refreshing or off-putting? Why?

Personally, His unvarnished expression of the truth appeals to me. I like knowing Jesus will shoot straight with me even if I find it uncomfortable!

If someone was evaluating your relationship with Jesus based solely on 1 John 1:6-10 (how quickly and completely you admit to being a sinner), do you think they'd describe you as being close to Him or distant from Him? Why?

The apostle Paul called himself the chief of sinners (see 1 Tim. 1:15). What title would you give yourself?

How would you describe the correlation between the *confession of sin* and the *feeling of freedom?*

scene five

RESPONSE (FROM GOD):

By saying that the LORD's table may
be despised. When you offer blind animals
in sacrifice, is that not evil?
And when you offer those that are
lame or sick, is that not evil?

Malachi 1:7c-8a

My favorite television show of all when I was growing up was *Mutual of Omaha's Wild Kingdom.* I especially loved the episodes where the host Marlin Perkins and his handsome, khaki-clad sidekick, Stan Brock, traveled to the wide-open plains of Africa to film regal golden lions; giant, gentle-seeming elephants; and those oddly graceful giraffes. Therefore when I got to go to Kenya a few years ago it was the fulfillment of a childhood dream.

The landscape was just as gorgeous as I'd imagined it would be and the animals were even more amazing than I'd hoped when I got to see them up close. But eclipsing both the scenery and the wildlife were the beautiful hearts of the African women with whom I got to rub shoulders. They welcomed our group with the kind of affectionate hugs usually reserved for soldiers returning home from a long war. They danced around us as if we were a Maypole covered with $100 bills. Every time we sat down to eat, they joyfully served us meat. Which in African households usually means they rung the neck of their one and only chicken that they'd been fattening up for months for a special occasion. It was humbling to realize that *we* were their special occasion.

Believe me, it was a hard fall when I arrived back on U.S. soil—in Newark, New Jersey, of all places—and walked up to

The word sacrifice refers to a peace offering in the Old Testament sacrificial system and expressed communion with God. burnt offerings expressed dedication to God.[4]

a fast-food counter in the airport. I was so happy to be off the plane after the 20-plus hour journey from Nairobi that I greeted the burger queen behind the counter with a smile and a friendly, "Hi, how are you?" But she was so preoccupied with her cell phone she didn't even look up. When I finally got her attention, she did *not* embrace me or dance around in joyful circles; instead she smacked her gum, rolled her eyes, and smirked. A few minutes later, she sullenly handed me a bag containing a cold sandwich and limp fries.

In light of the moldy bologna and brown bananas the priests were offering up in the temple, they didn't have any enthusiasm for their jobs either. Instead of happily frying up the fattest chickens in the churchyard for God, they were throwing greasy nuggets into paper bags and shoving them across the counter, not even looking up to acknowledge the King they were serving.

List some of the things the Israelites were told to do or not do regarding their offerings in Leviticus 22:1-3,21-22.

Did you note that offerings were to be presented with respect and only by a worshiper who was ceremonially clean? And the offered animals were to be unblemished and without defect. No blind, injured, maimed, or sick animal could be a sacrifice.

How do you think we give God "crippled animals" in modern Christian culture?

The passage in Leviticus makes clear that *both* the Israelites—by offering up scratch-and-dent sacrifices—and the priests—who were selling and accepting them—were mutually guilty of breaking God's law.

Do you think the priests' transgressions were more serious since they had been specifically chosen to be the spiritual leaders of Israel? Why or why not?

How does the New Testament underscore the responsibility of spiritual leadership in James 3:1 and 1 Timothy 3:1-7?

Although the James and Timothy verses seem to mandate a higher level of responsibility for spiritual leaders, in response to the 1 Timothy passage, theologian D.A. Carson notes that, "With the exception of only two qualifications [3:2 and 3:6], everything else in this list is elsewhere mandated of *all* Christians."[5]

So why do you think Christians tend to put pastors and priests on pedestals and then become outraged if they fall off?

scene six

IMPLICATION (TO ISRAEL):

Present that to your governor; will he
accept you or show you favor? says the
Lord of hosts. And now entreat the favor
of God, that he may be gracious to us.
With such a gift from your hand, will he
show favor to any of you? says the Lord of
hosts. Oh that there were one among you
who would shut the doors, that you might
not kindle fire on my altar in vain! I
have no pleasure in you, says the Lord of
hosts, and I will not accept an offering
from your hand. For from the rising of the
sun to its setting my name will be great
among the nations, and in every place
incense will be offered to my name, and a
pure offering. For my name will be great
among the nations, says the Lord of hosts.
But you profane it when you say that the
Lord's table is polluted, and its fruit,
that is, its food may be despised. But
you say, "What a weariness this is," and
you snort at it, says the Lord of hosts.

> You bring what has been taken by violence
> or is lame or sick, and this you bring as
> your offering! Shall I accept that from
> your hand? says the LORD. Cursed be the
> cheat who has a male in his flock, and vows
> it, and yet sacrifices to the Lord what is
> blemished. For I am a great King, says the
> LORD of hosts, and my name will be feared
> among the nations.
>
> Malachi 1:8b-14

When my dad Angel was in high school he and some of his buddies on the football team decided to pull a really foolish, only-teenage-boys-would-come-up-with-this prank. Late one Friday night after one of their games, they "borrowed" a mannequin from a local men's store, dressed him up in pajamas and a robe, and then placed him in the middle of the street where the road curved sharply.

They hid in the bushes on the side of the road to see what would happen and were thoroughly delighted when a grumpy, old spinster named Edna Bernstein (who'd yelled at most of the kids in town at one time or another) drove smack into their decoy, flattening the plastic man like a pancake. Of course, poor Miss Bernstein slammed on her brakes and squealed to a stop at which point Dad and his rambunctious posse took off sprinting for their respective homes.

Dad said they laughed so hard over the smashing success of their prank that they had to stop several times on the escape route to catch their breath. But he said he wasn't laughing at all the next morning when the local police chief knocked on his front door and asked his dad, "Is John Gordon home?"

When Dad stepped forward and said, "Yessir, I'm right here" Captain Perkins didn't say anything else. He just held up a man's bathrobe—which had big, black tire marks on it—and pointed to the name that was printed on the inside collar in indelible ink: *John Gordon Angel.*

One word described my dad's predicament: *Busted!* Which is exactly where the Israelite priests find themselves at the end of Malachi chapter 1 and the beginning of chapter 2; they were *busted.* Caught with their hands in the cookie jar.

How would you punish the Israelite priests if God made you chairman of the "Divine Consequences Committee"?

If you were writing a text message to *encourage* the Israelite priests, how would you use Galatians 6:7-9?

Pastor and author John Piper once said in a sermon, "The worst enemy of enthusiasm is time."[6] In addition to *time,* what else have you experienced that dampened your enthusiasm for God?

What are some of the practical, effective things you do to keep your enthusiasm for God burning bright?

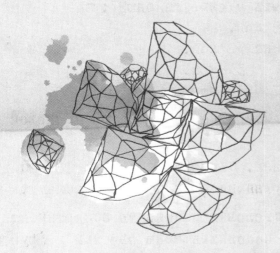

MINING PERSONAL JEWELS FROM MALACHI'S STORY

Write out Psalm 51:12 on two index cards and give one each to two people you consider safe, mature, long-term Christian friends. Ask them to prayerfully consider your life in light of this verse and then to write specific areas where they haven't observed as much joy in your walk of faith as they used to on the back of the card. Ask them to give the card back to you when they're done so you can pray about the areas they've observed your joy waning.

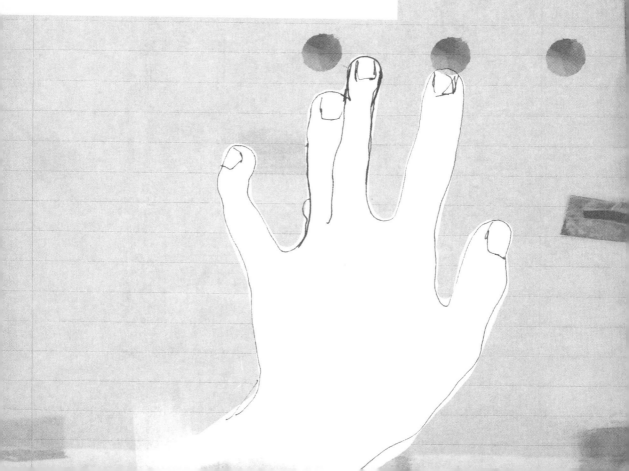

Treasure Hunt

1. Go through your closet and/or jewelry box and pick out a few items you still enjoy wearing and "sacrifice" them to the Salvation Army or a home-less shelter.

2. Begin a "No Crippled Cows Allowed" clothing and home goods campaign with your Bible study group and choose several ministries to give your haul of new and gently-used treasures to!

4. our Creator is a committed family Man

One Christmas Eve when I was 4 years old and my sister, Theresa, was 8 we had the conversation that strikes fear in the heart of parents everywhere.

THERESA: You know there's no such thing as Santa Claus, Leila. He's make-believe like the Easter Bunny or the Tooth Fairy.

ME: Un-uh.

THERESA: Uh-huh.

ME: 'Dat's not twue, Tare-wee.

THERESA: Yes it is because I stayed up all night on Christmas Eve last year to make sure, and it wasn't Santa who put our presents under the tree—it was Dad!

ME: I don't beweave you.

THERESA: Well then you're stupid because there's no such thing as Santa Claus or the North Pole, or elves, or flying reindeer! Plus, we don't even have a chimney so how do you think he gets into our house?

ME: *(Eyes widen. Tears well. Face crumples.)* Mama!

I don't remember what Mom said to console me, but I remember what happened that night. I was lying in bed, devastated by the knowledge that the whole Santa spiel—spunky Rudolph, the airborne sleigh, happy elves humming while creating toys—was a myth, when I heard something on the roof. At first I thought it was thunder, but quickly realized the sound was coming from someone, or some*thing,* stomping around over my head. Then it sounded like lots of little feet—hooves maybe—running around on the roof. Then I heard jingling bells. Finally I heard a hearty chuckle followed by "Ho, Ho, Ho … Merry Christmas!"

I shot out of bed, ran into the living room, and exclaimed that Santa Claus himself was ON. OUR. ROOF! To which Mom shrugged and said, "I told you he was real, Baby. Now go back to bed so he can put your presents under the tree." My faith in Santa was mostly restored for at least another year. It was many more years before I found out "Santa-on-the-roof" was actually my Aunt Darlene who came up with the sweet stunt and recruited some of her friends to pull it off because she didn't want my Christmas to be ruined. To this day, she's still my favorite aunt—just don't tell my Aunt Susan or Aunt Jeanette!

Then there was that fall weekend of my senior year in high school when my sister, a senior in college at the time, spent every dime she'd saved to buy a plane ticket home to surprise me when I was on homecoming court. Even though my dress flew briefly over my head—exposing my nether regions to a football stadium filled with people—when the queen contestants were driven around the track in a convertible; and even though my friend Wendy was crowned queen—relegating the rest of us to also-ran status—nothing could dampen my joy that Friday night because my sister had come just to sit in the stands and beam at me. She actually thought it was worth spending every penny she'd earned babysitting and skipping out on her own collegiate weekend festivities to fly home and cheer for younger sister!

Then there was the week last summer when my little brother, John Price, who lives in Florida, spent his vacation with me. He knew I was having a hard time dealing with Dad's death and the loss of a long-term friendship. So instead of going on one of his beloved fishing trips, he chose to hang out with me. We spent five days staining the deck, planting fruit trees, going on hikes, eating copious amounts of fried food, watching his favorite boy movies, and laughing until our sides ached.

J.P. also told story after sweet story about Dad. Like the time Dad found him playing with feathers soon after he'd gotten his first pellet gun for his 7th birthday. Dad said, "Son, where'd you get those?" After John confessed he'd killed a blue jay, Dad asked in a low, serious drawl, "Are you hungry, Son?" J.P. replied, "No sir," a bit perplexed by the question. Dad squatted down next to him and fiddled with the feathers for few seconds then said gently but firmly, "Don't kill another animal unless you plan to eat it," upon which he stood up, took my little brother by the hand, got a shovel from the garage, and walked back to where John shot the bird so they could give it a "proper burial."

Several times while listening to John reminisce about Dad, I was pulled back to the present when tears dripped off my chin. His stories triggered a rush of affection tinged with grief that I'd held back for a long time. Because Dad Angel wasn't always an ideal, loving stepfather, I've chosen to be intentional about processing in counseling the painful memories that involved him. It took years for me to come to terms with his misogyny and with the fact that most of the wounds he inflicted weren't deliberate. That he couldn't love me very well in light of the damage he lugged around from his childhood. What I didn't realize was that in rooting out all of the bad experiences I had with Dad Angel, I'd inadvertently wiped out the good times too.

I'd almost forgotten how he patiently taught me to cast a rod and reel in our backyard. How he always whistled when puttering in his shop or working on the boat. How he used to ask, "Do you know how a horse bites an apple?" Then he'd reach over and grab the ticklish spot just above my knee. How he was there too at that homecoming game 30 years ago. Although he didn't beam proudly like my sister, there was a faint smile on his face as he escorted me awkwardly across the field. My Aunt Darlene, sister Theresa, tender-hearted little brother John Price, Mom Patti, Dad Harper, and even my Dad Angel are beautiful colors in the tapestry of *family* our Heavenly Father has woven me into.

Whether you come from an intact, mostly-loving family or from a frayed, more dysfunctional fabric like mine, remember that family was God's design from the beginning of time. Therefore it has divine *value*. Which is what He's trying to explain to Malachi's rebellious peers in the next passage we're going to dive into.

video notes:

_____

_____

_____

_____

_____

_____

_____

_____

_____

1. Name three people you'd walk through blood for. Name three people who'd walk through blood for you.

2. Along with illuminating that God thinks we're worth dying for, what else does the blood covenant point to?

3. Read Hebrews 9:11-14. When did you come to believe Jesus' blood on the cross paved the way?

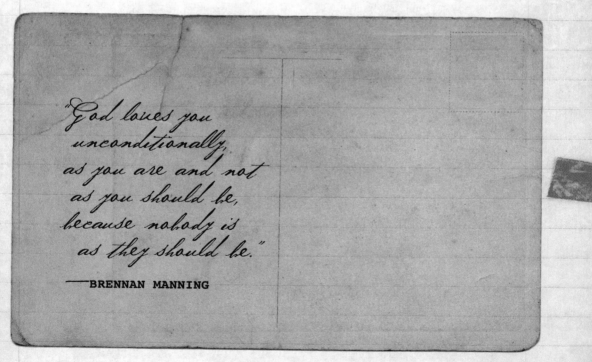

"God loves you unconditionally, as you are and not as you should be, because nobody is as they should be."

——BRENNAN MANNING

Brennan Manning, *All Is Grace* (Colorado Springs, CO: David C Cook, 2011), 192.

scene 1
assertion (from Malachi): Malachi 2:10-13

scene 2
questioning (from Israel): Malachi 2:14a

scene 3
response (from Malachi): Malachi 2:14b

scene 4
implication (to Israel): Malachi 2:10-16

how is my faith in God demonstrated
by how I love my family?

SETTING THE STAGE

My eyes are bigger than my stomach when it comes to fall deco-
rating. During the first week or so of October, I'll drive by one of
those darling pumpkin displays—the ones crowded with young
dads balancing babies on top of giant orange orbs while moms
try to get the perfect picture. And when I drive by those squash
superstores I can't help but pull over.

    I get out of the car and begin walking through row after row
of ginger-colored goodness. Voices in my head whisper things
like, *I need just a* few *more pumpkins to make my fall display perfect. You know it would be so nice to have displays at the front
and the back door to make guests feel welcome coming and
going.* Followed by the codependent clincher, *I really should put
a display at the end of the driveway to help make motorists on
Highway 46 feel happier when they zoom past.* Then like those
crazed women in Christmas sweaters who maniacally stuff their
carts full of waffle irons and fondue machines every Black Friday,
I gleefully load up my SUV with unnecessary pumpkins.

    The problem with my gourd-hoarding is it doesn't take long
in Tennessee's typically mild fall weather for pumpkins to go from
plump to slump and for my cheerful displays to deteriorate into
something sad and saggy. Usually by Halloween, I have to start
repositioning the pumpkins daily so the slack sides are in back
and they still look presentable. By the first week of November,
they've deteriorated so much that all I'm left with is a bunch of
rotten fruit all folded in on itself. A veritable pumpkin graveyard.
Which translates into several hundred pounds of disgusting goo I
have to figure out how to cart and carry off to the dump.

    In Malachi's time, something infinitely worse than seasonal
decor had begun to deteriorate in Israel. The very foundation of
their culture started folding in on itself. A once-beautiful display
of their covenant with Yahweh turned into a marital graveyard as
Jewish husbands turned away from their wives in divorce—tearing holes in the fabric of family and leaving the youngest generation of God's people to wonder anxiously about which parent
they'd spend Passover with.

INTRODUCING NEW CHARACTERS

Like males in midlife crises all over the world, some of the guys in Malachi's generation were dissatisfied with their jobs, dissatisfied with their income, dissatisfied with their inability to throw a football like they used to (or how they bragged they used to), and most of all, dissatisfied with the wives of their youth (see Mal. 2:14). So their eyes began to wander.

Now in all fairness, their wives probably had gotten a little wider through the hips, what with all the carbs in the cheap food they'd had to subsist on since returning home to Jerusalem from Babylon. Plus, since their men were at the low end of the pay scale, they couldn't afford to replace the bald tires on the family minivan or buy their kids new shoes for school, much less get the highlights and lowlights their hair so desperately needed. Which sometimes left them in a bad mood, which they often took out on their husbands.

My guess is those Jewish housewives weren't exactly the easiest girls in the world to be yoked to! Therefore the next person to walk on stage in Israel's postexilic drama is the ancient version of what we now call second wives.

One can only assume they were younger and hotter and seemingly less grumpy than the Israelite gals. Based on recorded history, we *know* they were pagans—they had absolutely no relationship with God. However that didn't matter to the jerkiest husbands in Judah because they were only motivated by two things: sex and money. The sex part is clear.

The money part involved the possibility of gaining favor with foreign father-in-laws, with Philistine and Ammonite and Moabite daddies. Because in light of the fact those men were the landowners of fifth-century B.C. Judah, some of Malachi's pigheaded peers viewed them as winning lottery tickets.

scene one

ASSERTION (FROM MALACHI):

Have we not all one Father? Has not one God created us? Why then are we faithless to one another, profaning the covenant of our fathers? Judah has been faithless. …

You cover the LORD's altar with tears, with weeping and groaning because he no longer regards the offering or accepts it with favor from your hand. Malachi 2:10-13

This passage is actually three assertions rolled into one—God is calling His people on the carpet for interfaith marriage (see vv. 10-12); for emotive, pagan style worship (see vv. 12-13); and for quickie, no-fault divorces (see vv. 14-16). The passage starts out with two poetic couplets (see v. 10) and changes to full-on prose for the rest of God's rebuke (see vv. 11-16). Since most poetry in Near Eastern language was musical, scholars suggest that Malachi sang the beginning of this disputation.[1] If that's the case, I think Malachi probably sounded like Merle Haggard here because this is a pretty sad song.

The Greek term JEW historically refers to a member of the tribe of Judah. The Israelites came to be commonly known as "Jews/Jewish" during the postexilic era—fifth-century B.C.—in regard to how they'd returned home from Babylon to inhabit the land of Judah.

The first lyrics emphasize the fatherhood of God and His unique relationship with the Israelites. Don't forget they started out as total Teacher's pets. God literally created them to be *His people*. He'd given them the best seat on the planet, pulled out an ornate chair chosen especially for them, and lit up the universe with a smile when they sat down to dine with Him. Yet instead of being grateful, God's people chose to put their elbows on the table, push their food around on their plate, and covertly text other beaus on the phones in their laps. They simply couldn't wait to sneak away from God's affection, to shatter His covenant and date other people.

Why do you suppose we humans seem so inclined to become bored with what we once longed for and begin looking at the greener grass on the other side of the fence?

How does this "relational boredom" factor play out for you? What fence line poses a temptation for you? Note that temptation is different for each of us, but Satan doesn't seem to spare anyone from it.

One of the saddest stories I read while poring through commentaries about this passage was in Dr. James Montgomery Boice's commentary on the Minor Prophets. He tells the true story of Mark Twain's marriage to Olivia Langdon. Miss Langdon was raised by committed Christian parents and was a devoted follower of Jesus Christ by the time Mr. Twain came courting. Since he was an outspoken critic of religion, their union seemed unlikely. However, Olivia eventually accepted his proposal, no doubt hoping that his heart would soften toward God. At first, her hopes seemed to be coming true when her young husband began taking part in family prayers and Bible reading.

Unfortunately Mark Twain's skepticism about matters of faith ultimately won the battle for his heart and he's quoted as saying, "Livy, you may keep this up if you want to, but I must ask you to excuse me from it. It is making me a hypocrite. I don't believe in the Bible; it contradicts my reason."[2] And while the reality of this great American writer's hardened heart toward Christianity is sad, what happened to Olivia's relationship with Jesus is even sadder. Because when she was mourning someone's death a few years later and Twain encouraged her to lean on her Christian faith if it would help her, she replied, "I can't, Youth [her favorite designation for her husband]. I haven't any."[3]

God isn't some fuddy-duddy trying to limit our dating pool. He's a loving Father who grieves when His people choose to marry unbelievers because He knows we will likely be pulled away from Him in the process. Therefore He regarded the Israelite's weeping and wailing at the altar as insincere crocodile tears (see v. 13). He knew their loyalty was limited once they placed a diamond ring on a pagan partner.

Read Genesis 1:26-27. How do you think the fact that our Creator Redeemer is a Trinitarian God—a community unto Himself, who exists in _ontological equality_—imprints us with regard to relationships?

Ontology is the study of being. Ontological equality means the three members of the Trinity are equal in their being.[4]

What deterrents did Nehemiah (Malachi's contemporary) use to combat the problem of interfaith marriages in postexilic Israel in Nehemiah 13:23-27?

How would you encourage your children or close friends not to marry someone who doesn't have a real relationship with Jesus?

How would you explain the difference between the *ethnic intermarriage* that Ruth and Boaz shared (see Ruth 4:9-10), which God blessed, with the *religious intermarriage* Solomon had with so many of his wives (see 1 Kings 11:1-6), which made God angry?

Read Psalm 42 and 1 Kings 18:26-30. When does weeping during worship come across as insincere to you? When does it ring true?

scene two

QUESTIONING (FROM ISRAEL):

But you say, "Why does he not?"

Malachi 2:14a

One of my friends went through a divorce from his wife when she left him for another man after years of painful and often public promiscuity on her part. While he was devastated, she zoomed merrily away from their union like she'd just swung through a drive-thru for a Diet Coke and was headed back to the highway. In fact, the only time she slowed down was when a court order was issued preventing her from letting their young children spend the night at her lover's house so as to keep them from being exposed to excess alcohol consumption and pornography. She seemed shocked by judge's decision and then asked one of the dumbest questions I've ever heard given her situation: "Why?"

The Israelites were as obtuse as my friend's ex-wife. Here they'd trampled all over their marriage vows, not to mention their covenant with Yahweh. They'd snuck out in the middle of the night and come home with lipstick on their collar. They'd siphoned from their meager savings accounts for cheap perfume and Chinese take-out. They spent Saturday afternoons hung over with illicit lovers in seedy motels instead of cheering at their kids' soccer games. Yet when the God of the Universe—who *sees everything*—tells them their behavior is deplorable, they cock their heads to the side, turn their hands palms up, and feign innocence by asking, "What are You talking about, Abba?"

How would you synopsize 2 Corinthians 7:10 into a movie or book title?

Describe a situation when you were little and you pretended to be innocent of the "crime" your parents were punishing you for.

When's the last time you feigned innocence when your Heavenly Father convicted you of doing something wrong? Describe that situation.

What are some of the most effective ways you've found to stay aware of what's going on in your own heart?

In Genesis 1:20-24 when no suitable companion was found for Adam among all the living things God had created, He fashioned Eve out of one of Adam's ribs to which Adam responded, "This at last is bone of my bones and flesh of my flesh; she shall be called Woman, because she was taken out of Man" (Gen. 2:23). This story not only proves that women legitimately have a bone to pick with men, it establishes the divine foundation of marriage!

scene three

RESPONSE (FROM MALACHI):

Because the LORD was witness between you
and the wife of your youth, to whom you
have been faithless, though she is your
companion and your wife by covenant.

Malachi 2:14b

Outside of reality television and certain parts of Utah and Nevada, polygamy isn't practiced in modern culture. However in Old Testament times, polygamy was universal. First marriages were normally arranged and planned for children long before puberty—sometimes before the husband and bride-to-be were even born. Then in anticipation of the future coupling, both sets of parents made a binding contract officially declaring their children's betrothal. After that *first* marriage ceremony took place years or perhaps decades later, the groom was free to marry other women. But those women were subjugated as *noninheriting* wives (see Judg. 19:1) or *other* wives (see Gen. 4:19; Deut. 21:15; 1 Sam. 1:2) and didn't have the distinction of being the first wife. Neither did any subsequent marriage give men the right to divorce "the wife of [his] youth."

Unlike our society where people often see marriage as just a pit stop on the way to some utopian romantic pipe dream, marriage then was a serious *covenant.* It was intended to be a genuine 'til-death-do-us-part promise. Furthermore most Old Testament newlyweds had lots of friends and family members committed to help them stay true to their vows.

There weren't too many ancient mother-in-laws sniping about their daughter-in-law's cooking or father-in-laws smirking about their son-in-law's inability to tune a transmission because arranged marriages were often the result of two clans forming a union so as to increase their collective wealth and power. Which meant it was definitely in the best interest of *both* families for young couples to stay together.

More importantly, in Jewish families, marriage was understood to be a subcovenant of the overarching covenant Yahweh made with them (see Ex. 19; Deut. 33). So in effect, to walk away from their promise to "have and to hold from this day forward" in marriage, was to walk away from all the pentateuchal promises God had made with them centuries before. Tossing aside their first wife for a newer model with more bells and whistles was akin to thumbing their nose at the Creator of the Universe.

Genesis 31:44-50 tells of the covenant between Jacob and Laban. They set up a monument as a reminder that the "Lord watch between you and me, when we are out of one another's sight" (v. 49).

How would you describe the significance of God being the *implicit witness* of every promise we make?

If you literally had to have a face-to-face conversation with God prior to breaking any promise you've made, how often do you think you'd cancel your commitments?

Think about the last time you got to *witness* a couple making vows of holy matrimony or a new believer making vows of faith in Jesus Christ.

What responsibility, if any, do you think is incumbent upon those who witnessed vows being made when the person/ people who made the vows they witnessed is in jeopardy of breaking them?

Describe the following firsts:

your first crush

your first kiss

your first paycheck

your first Christmas in your own house or apartment

Were most of those "firsts" sweet? If you could go back in time and change them, would you? Why or why not, and if so, how?

Read Jeremiah 31:31-33. What has God *written on your heart* recently that encouraged you to be faithful in your relationship with Him?

scene four

IMPLICATION (TO ISRAEL):

Did he not make them one, with a portion of the Spirit in their union? … So guard yourselves in your spirit, and do not be faithless. Malachi 2:15-16

Many have felt the phrase "God hates divorce" like a club beating them for their status. The HCSB and ESV translations reflect a more accurate treatment of the tricky grammar and linguistics with an "if-then" implication: *if* a man doesn't love his wife and chooses to divorce her *then* he covers his garment with violence.[5] Malachi's words clearly put the responsibility on the men divorcing their wives rather than simply condemning divorced people.

Of course, no matter which way you slice this passage, it's crystal clear that our Heavenly Father is opposed to divorce. I just feel the need to clarify the fact that God doesn't hate *people* who've had their hearts bruised in the break-up of a marriage because that's the story of my family.

In light of the provisions in Mosaic law for divorce and remarriage, theologians have speculated that having no provision for divorce might have increased domestic violence and abandonment in Jewish culture, without giving women any hope of another marriage. Furthermore, the provision limiting a man's right to remarry the wife he divorced could both cause him to think more seriously before divorcing in the first place and prevent a return to an abusive situation.

As I mentioned earlier, my parents went through a divorce when I was a little girl. Their split did not resemble the amicable ones depicted on televisions sitcoms nowadays. They did not remain friends or go on vacations together with their new spouses or trade teasing comments about the way things used to be. On the contrary, it was an ugly and violent shredding of the promises they made to God and each other.

Unfortunately, as both of my parents would admit, the damage didn't stop when a judge granted their divorce decree. Instead it was the white elephant gift that kept on giving. Dad married the woman who'd captured his wandering eye and moved away to fulfill his fantasy of becoming a successful rancher.

Much like the Israelite men who married Philistine, Ammonite, and Moabite girls, my dad thought he'd finally hit the jackpot. But his dream turned to dust several years later when my stepmother left him for our veterinarian. While Mom stayed married to Dad Angel until he passed away last year, it was an often difficult relationship partly because of his stubborn agnosticism. We were overjoyed when he earnestly put his hope in Jesus 8 weeks before he died, but of course by then Mama had endured her own 40 years in the wilderness. Suffice it to say, the ripple effects of my parents' break-up buffeted our lives long after they walked away from their vows.

Clearly broken vows and divided families are heartbreaking. But consider with me the larger picture around this topic in Scripture. First Moses allowed divorce under certain conditions. Read Deuteronomy 24:1-4.

What are some of the results that might happen if Moses had refused to allow any legal process for divorce?

What possible effects could you imagine coming from the seemingly-odd provision limiting the right to remarry a wife after divorcing her?

What do you see as the difference between *permitting* and *regulating* divorce?

People usually cite Matthew 5:32; 19:9; Mark 10:11-12; and Luke 16:18 to prove that adultery is the only factor giving Christians biblical grounds for divorce. However God's Word *and* His grace must shape and guide our understanding of marriage and divorce. Even the theologically conservative, centuries-old Westminster Confession of Faith—a doctrinal standard of orthodoxy—reflects that divorce should be granted for at least *two* reasons: adultery and irreconcilable desertion. "Although the corruption of man be such as is apt to study arguments unduly to put asunder those whom God hath joined together in marriage: yet, nothing but adultery, or such willful desertion as can no way be remedied by the Church, or civil magistrate, is cause sufficient of dissolving the bond of marriage: wherein, a public and orderly course of proceeding is to be observed; and the persons concerned in it not left to their own wills and discretion in their own case."[6]

Our Redeemer isn't some cosmic killjoy who gets His jollies out of making people feel guilty about their relational mistakes. He's a loving Father who grieves over the emotional and spiritual trauma caused when we are unfaithful to each other and in so doing, unfaithful to Him. Divorce breaks His holy heart because of the way it divides our families, erodes our security, and destroys our communion with Him.

God didn't establish standards for marital stability to be punitive; He established them for *our good.* Praise God divorce isn't part of His perfect plan for mankind because if it was—if His attitude was "When the going gets tough, feel free to bail out"—we'd all be up the world's deepest creek without a paddle. Because surely God would've left our prone-to-wander selves when the honeymoon was over. Yet in spite of the fact that we've been a less-than-loyal bride, He stays.

Malachi uses two titles for God in verse 16: "the LORD, the God of Israel" and "the LORD of hosts" (which is a military title, emphasizing His absolute lordship in the battle of good and evil). Which of these titles makes you feel more secure and why?

Read Isaiah 43:1-4; 54:4-5. What adjectives would you use to describe our relationship with God in light of these verses? When did you first sense God calling you "Mine"?

MINING PERSONAL JEWELS FROM MALACHI'S STORY

Write a love note to your spouse (if you're married) and at least two other family members, which includes a list of things you appreciate most about them. Leave the note, along with a small gift that has personal significance to them, in a place where they're sure to find it.

Write a letter to one of your friends or family members who's in a pending-divorce or post-divorce situation. Without taking sides or offering counsel, simply communicate your hope that they will experience God's comfort and peace in the midst of their pain.

If you're married, plan and execute a special date night with your husband. It *cannot* involve eating dinner at a chain restaurant or going to a movie in a theater where you can't talk to each other! It *can* involve having a picnic in the park, taking a long walk around a lake, or lying on a blanket under the stars in your own backyard.

Date Night

1. **Schedule** an unbreakable date night with God on your calendar sometime during the next month.
2. **Carve** out at least two hours to be *alone with Him* one evening in a place that's conducive for private worship.

5. when divine grace masquerades as discipline

One of my oldest and dearest friends (from back in the day when we both had tight skin and high metabolisms, long before Facebook or Twitter) is a woman named Eva Whittington Self. She's got a razor sharp wit, a strong Southern accent, a generous heart, two beautiful daughters, and a dear Circuit Court Judge named Andrew for a husband (who I'm proud to say I've never asked to get me out of a traffic ticket!).

Eva is prone to profound spiritual insights and has counseled me toward Jesus and away from foolish choices on numerous occasions. She can also cook me under the table and beat me on the tennis court. Frankly, the only arena in which I'm "faster" than Eva is a footrace because she's been confined to a wheelchair since a car accident when she was 17 years old.

I used to hate her wheelchair because it reminded me of how she'd been hurt. Every time I heard the motorized ramp in her van I cringed inwardly, wishing she could just open her door and hop out like me instead of having to wait for that robotic arm to morph into a slope on which she could roll out of her vehicle.

I was so troubled by all the hardships of her everyday life—the maneuvering in and out of spaces that don't accommodate the chair; the exasperating searches for elevators in barely accessible buildings; the being ignored by clerks who act as if a person with paralyzed legs must be mentally and hearing impaired too—that one afternoon at the mall, I just snapped.

I plopped down on a bench next to Eva and burst into tears. I told her how sorry I was that she was stuck in a wheelchair. That she didn't deserve to suffer the way she did.

She smiled until I quit blubbering, then replied, "Lisa, I used to hate this chair too. But I don't anymore. This chair has taken me to places I never would've been otherwise. It's allowed me to meet incredible people and do incredible things I never would've done if I'd stayed in Concord, North Carolina. I wouldn't have married Andrew or had Abby and Audrey if it weren't for my accident. Sometimes I feel overwhelmed at the amazing things God has done for me through this chair. I stay overwhelmed over the fact that He thought I was worthy of this chair."

While I was still picking my chin up off the floor over how she considers life in a wheelchair a *privilege,* Eva told me a story about how grace can masquerade as difficulty and discipline. She described the week she came home from the rehab hospital. When she should've been shopping for a prom dress and deciding which graduation parties to attend, she was instead relearning the basics of personal hygiene—how to go to the bathroom, how to wash herself to ward off infections, and how to keep from sitting too long in one position so she wouldn't get pressure sores.

Eva described how one morning that week, in the sleepy haze of waking up, she didn't remember that her spine had been severed in an automobile wreck on an icy road. How for just a few sweet seconds, she was a carefree senior in high school again. But then she rubbed the sleep from her eyes and noticed something strange sitting in the corner of her bedroom and the harsh reality of her new life assaulted her senses when she recognized it was a wheelchair.

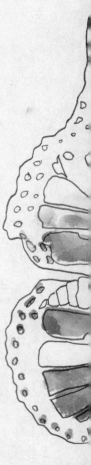

Eva said she thought about killing herself that day. However, one dawn soon afterward, God shifted Eva's heart and mind 180 degrees. On *that* morning her mother, May Bell Whittington, announced it was time for her to learn to put on her blue jeans by herself. Eva told her mom she was looking forward to the day she could dress herself too but they hadn't gotten to that part yet in occupational therapy and she still needed help.

May Bell—normally a timid and very tenderhearted woman— stood her ground and gently insisted that Eva needed to put on her own pants. Eva said she's embarrassed by the things she screamed at her mama then—how she vented her anger and bitterness on the one person who would've gladly traded places with her if she could have. But her mom didn't bite back. She simply stretched out the jeans on the bed so they'd be within her only daughter's reach and walked softly out of the room.

Eva said she was so furious that her mom "abandoned" her in her hour of need that she threw herself back on the mattress and began to sob. A little while later—when her mama didn't return to rescue her—she sat up and reached down and grabbed the waistband of the jeans and slowly began working her floppy feet into the pant legs. She said it took her 15 minutes just to get both feet into the right and left holes. After which, she fell back on the bed and cried again. Later—when her mama didn't return to rescue her—she sat up and wrestled with the jeans another 15 minutes to work them up to her knees. Then she fell back on the bed and cried some more. Awhile later—when her mama didn't return to rescue her—she sat up and began tugging those stiff Levi's toward her hips. Fifteen or so minutes later, she fell back onto the bed sweaty and exhausted. She said she was so spent she didn't even have the energy to cry anymore. Then—after her mama *still* didn't return to rescue her—Eva sat up one last time and inch by inch painstakingly worked her jeans up over her bulky back brace and finally buttoned them with a sigh.

Then, when she collapsed on her bed the last time with a victorious "Yes," she heard her mama crying. May Bell had been in the next room the whole time. It nearly broke her heart to listen to Eva struggle, but she loved her child way too much to rescue her. She wisely understood that Eva's path to physical independence would include pain. That to do everything for her would be to truly cripple her. So May Bell went against her mothering instincts and allowed her baby to battle, knowing that like a butterfly working its way out of a chrysalis, the fight was necessary.

Eva's beautiful metamorphosis from self-centered entitlement to God-centered gratitude reminds me of what I've heard my friend Sheila say on several occasions, "Some of God's best gifts come wrapped in boxes that make our hands bleed when we open them." In other words, divine grace often masquerades as difficulty and discipline. Such is the case in the next part of Malachi's story.

video notes:

_____

_____

_____

_____

_____

_____

_____

_____

_____

God's discipline is always braided with mercy.

1. What's the sweetest discipline you've received from your Heavenly Father?

2. If you haven't read Eva's story, read it now on pages 105-107. Who's a May Bell in your life, someone who loved you too much to rescue you? How did this May Bell love you enough to let you struggle?

> "God's wrath is not a cranky explosion, but his settled opposition to the cancer ... which is eating out the insides of the human race he loves with his whole being."
>
> —BECKY PIPPERT

Becky Pippert in Timothy Keller, *The Reason For God* (New York: Dutton, 2008), 73.

scene 1
assertion (from Malachi): Malachi 2:17a

scene 2
questioning (from Israel): Malachi 2:17b

scene 3
response (from Malachi): Malachi 2:17c

scene 4
implication (to Israel): Malachi 3:1-5

since God disciplines those He loves, why do
I resist His "rod" so much?

SETTING THE STAGE

A huge difference lies between pursuing God's heart and seeking gifts from His hands. Between feeling sincerely grateful for divine blessings and feeling like you *deserve* to be blessed. The self-centered attitude the Israelites have adopted by this fourth disputation puts them squarely in the second category; they were demanding goody bags from God and assumed they were *entitled* to them. Whenever entitlement rears its ugly head, you can be sure it's not alone because like Bonnie and Clyde, entitlement and insecurity always travel as a team.

(On a side note: I think it's imperative for God's people to learn that insecurity is *not* the opposite of arrogance. Frankly insecurity and arrogance are fruit from the same tree. Christians who wear wounded feelings on their sleeve, who are quick to take offense, and who reek of anxiety are *not* humble. They're trust-impaired. The true opposite of arrogance is *security.* It's the deep-seated confidence that God holds us in the palm of His hand and nothing can separate us from His love.)

Now back to the main stage: when the Israelite's hope rested in the supernatural goodness of their Creator, they were overcomers. They made it to the promised land, tired and parched but happy to finally have a place to call home. They survived Babylon, bruised but not beaten. However when they trekked to Canaan a second time only to discover it in total disarray, doubt hijacked their can-do attitudes. Instead of turning *to* God for help, they turned *on* God with more insecurity than a middle school girl scorned. They drooped their heads dejectedly on their desks during homeroom and between classes whispered about whether or not He was treating them as good as they deserved. They crossed through His name on their notebooks with dramatic huffs. But then, right before they shove themselves into a locker of bitterness, God passes them a love note through Malachi.

INTRODUCING NEW CHARACTERS

Because one of my sorority sisters (Tammy Watford) had a walk-on role in the 1994 movie *Nell,* I went to see it the day it opened in theaters across the country. From the first scene, I was transfixed and sat with my eyes glued to the screen, partly because I was scanning for Tammy's image but mostly because I've always been fascinated by stories of a feral child raised by wild animals (like *The Jungle Book, The Wild Boy of Aveyron,* and *Tarzan of the Apes).* The plotline of this particular movie borrowed heavily from that genre.

It went something like this: a handsome and compassionate doctor (played by Liam Neeson) discovers a childlike woman named "Nell" (played by Jodie Foster) living in a shack deep in the woods of North Carolina. Nell and her twin sister May, who died in childhood, were raised in total isolation by their mother, who conceived the twins after she had been violently raped and was incapacitated by a stroke when they were little. Therefore, Nell, who'd had no contact with anyone besides May and her mom—who was also deceased by the time Dr. Lovell found Nell—speaks in a barely discernible dialect (an *idioglossia)* that she and May created by mimicking their mom's garbled speech.

And much like the pivotal, tearjerking scene in *The Miracle Worker* when Anne Sullivan teaches Helen Keller the word "water," there's an aha moment in *Nell* when Dr. Lovell realizes the word *eva-dur,* that Nell keeps repeating when refusing to leave her cabin at night, actually means "evil-doer." In a misguided attempt to keep Nell safe, the term was the word her mama taught her from the Bible to describe people in the outside world.

The same nefarious characters Nell was afraid of—evildoers—are the ostensibly new characters in this fourth disputation of Malachi. Of course, the Israelites are referring to non-Jewish antagonists here; people who were openly opposing Yahweh in fifth-century B.C. by their wicked deeds and idolatrous worship. But what God's chosen people didn't notice was that while they were pointing an accusing finger at the Moabites, Edomites, Ammonites, and a host of other "ites," they had three fingers pointing back at themselves.

scene one

Unfortunately this moment in Malachi isn't unique. God's people have often wearied Him by wobbling in whiney insecurity instead of standing confidently in the assurance of His sovereign compassion:

Surely Job exasperated the Almighty when he challenged His sense of fairness.

JOB REPLIED: "I'm not letting up—I'm standing my ground. My complaint is legitimate. God has no right to treat me like this—it isn't fair! If I knew where on earth to find him, I'd go straight to him. I'd lay my case before him face-to-face, give him all my arguments firsthand. I'd find out exactly what he's thinking, discover what's going on in his head. Do you think he'd dismiss me or bully me? No, he'd take me seriously. He'd see a straight-living man standing before him; my Judge would acquit me for good of all charges."
Job 23:1-7, Message

Can you think of a time when someone has "wearied you" with their words? Children, spouses, and friends are all possible candidates. Please tell me a little about how it felt without dishonoring or identifying the persons involved.

OK, you knew I was going to do this. What about you? Can you describe a time when you've petulantly exasperated someone else—possibly even God—with *your* words?

The list of how I've exasperated my friends—and surely God—with my words is a pretty long one. So I'm not surprised by the numerous word-weary incidents in Scripture. Can't you just picture God shaking His holy head back and forth and sighing when immediately after the miracle He rained down on Mount Carmel, His prophet Elijah turned tail and fled to the dessert because he allowed a bully named Jezebel usurp his faith.

Read 1 Kings 19:1-4. If you had been God at that moment, how do you think you would have responded to Elijah?

When I was growing up and burdened my mama the way Job, Elijah, and Malachi's buddies burdened their Heavenly Father, she'd walk out into the backyard, pick a switch off the cherry tree, come back inside, and tell me to lie facedown on my bed. Then she'd earnestly say, "This is going to hurt me more than it's going to hurt you," before giving me a few whacks.

I find it amazing that our Redeemer rarely spanks even His most wearisome kids. Although we must get on God's very last nerve, He continues to respond to us with mercy. I'm so glad that Numbers 14:18 describes God as "slow to anger and rich in faithful love" (HCSB) and Psalm 86:15 describes Him as "compassionate and gracious" (HCSB).

What recent, personal example can you think of that reflects God's compassion and graciousness?

How do you do respond when it comes to accepting God's compassion for yourself? Do you have an easier time believing in God's love and mercy for other people than you do for yourself?

Think of a friend who's repented of a huge mistake (such as being convicted of a crime or having an affair). Now on the following scale put an X on the spot that shows how completely you believe God has forgiven him or her for their offense.

completely
forgiven

still working
on forgiveness

Now think of something you've done in the past year or two that fell short of God's expectations. Draw a stick figure on the same scale to represent where you see yourself.

What does this grace and mercy scale reveal about the way you view yourself and other people with regard to God's compassion?

Isaiah 43:22-24 expresses a fascinating combination of feelings on God's part. On the one hand He says Israel didn't care enough about Him to bring their worship and offerings. On the other hand, they wearied Him with their sins.

Why do you suppose we can put up with someone's shortcomings more easily if we know they really care about us?

When are you prone to feel weary in your walk of faith? Do you tend to be more vocal about your spiritual burdens, like Malachi's peers and Job, or do you try to run away from them, like Elijah?

In the fruit of the Spirit passage, the word translated "patience" (Gal. 5:22) is *makrothymia*, which comes from the Greek root words *macro* (meaning *large, great,* or *long*) and *thermia* (meaning *heat*).[1] Therefore, the New Testament picture of patience is when it takes someone a long time to get hot!

When have you been aware recently that God was taking a long time to get hot with you?

Do you think your friends and family would describe you as having a short temper or a long temper? Has your temper gotten shorter or longer in the past few years? Explain why you think it's shortened or lengthened.

scene two

QUESTIONING (FROM ISRAEL):

But you say, "How have we wearied him?"

Malachi 2:17b

If Malachi was anything like me, he probably wanted to slap the Israelites upside the head and give them a big piece of his mind. If I was him, I think I would've grabbed their scrawny shoulders, shook them as hard as I could, and yelled: "How have you wearied Yahweh?! Well, for starters you've been acting like a bunch of babies ever since we got home from Babylon. All you do is whine and complain, whine and complain. Now you have the audacity to ask *how* you've exhausted Him? Good night, it's a wonder He doesn't zap you fatheads with a lightening bolt!"

One of my favorite saints of old is Thomas á Kempis. In *Of the Imitation of Christ,* he wrote a warning that pertains to situations like this: "What have you, O vain man, to complain of? What can you answer, foul sinner, to them that upbraid you, you who have so often offended God, and so many times deserved Hell?"[2]

Instead of asking, "What did we do to make you mad, Yahweh?" Malachi's peers should've been facedown on the floor crying, "We need your mercy, oh God!" Which is the posture I need to be in more often too, being that I'm a foul sinner *and* a fathead.

How long does it typically take you to get hot with people who've wronged you but won't admit it?

Exodus 32 contains the key Israelite event of the golden calf. When Moses hiked up Mount Sinai to receive the Ten Commandments, the people complained to his brother. Aaron quickly buckled and came up with a crazy, heretical scheme to appease them. He instructed the Israelites to bring him their gold, and then he shaped it into a shiny, bovine idol. Aaron even had the audacity to declare, "Israel, this is your God, who brought you up from the land of Egypt!" (v. 4, HCSB).

When Moses confronted Aaron, he immediately threw the Israelites under the bus and came up with the prototype for all excuses: "They said to me, 'Make us gods who shall go before us. As for this Moses, the man who brought us up out of the land of Egypt, we do not know what has become of him.' So I said to them, 'Let any who have gold take it off.' So they gave it to me, and I threw it into the fire, and out came this calf" (vv. 23-24).

How does the Israelites' response to being accused of wearying God by Malachi remind you of their forefather Aaron's excuse when Moses accused him of idolatry?

Share an example of when you tried to distance yourself from the responsibility of wrongdoing by asking your accuser a question or changing the subject. If you have children, share an example of when they told a fantastical lie like Aaron—"I tossed some watches into the fireplace and *shazam,* a gold cow popped out!"—to get out of trouble.

scene three

RESPONSE (FROM MALACHI):

By saying, "Everyone who does evil is good
in the sight of the LORD, and he delights
in them." Or by asking, "Where is the God
of justice?" Malachi 2:17c

Good old Malachi sees right through the Israelite's desperate ploy to throw God off track and cover up their culpability. So he whips out his iPhone and plays a video he shot of them raising their fists toward Heaven and hurling these complaints: "Why are pagans cruising around in BMWs while we're stuck driving these rusted-out Chevys? How come the Babylonians get to live in huge houses with stainless steel appliances and granite countertops and built-in swimming pools while we have to live in these nasty, government-subsidized apartments with no air-conditioning, much less a pool? What were you thinking, Abba, letting them go on lavish vacations while just giving us these trashy T-shirts? This isn't fair, Yahweh! We're your chosen people so *we deserve to be treated better than this!*"

The heretical belief behind their egocentric hissy fit wasn't simply that Yahweh was being inequitable, it's that everyone who was doing *evil* was perceived as *good* in His eyes. They were literally calling into question the perfect nature of the Creator and Sustainer of the Universe. In other words, the very people God chose to be on His all-star team were stomping off the court and accusing *Him* of cheating!

Old Testament Commentator Thomas Edward McComiskey sums up the outrageous impudence of the Israelites (as well as modern-day believers) like this: "Sinners are invariably inconsistent. The thief is always outraged when someone steals from *him.* The liar is deeply offended when someone lies to *her.* The cheater deeply resents finding that *she* has been defrauded, and the murderer wants *himself* and his family to live in peace."[3]

I'm ashamed to admit how well Dr. McComiskey's summation fits me. I suppose there is always a hypocrite lurking in the closets of a critical spirit.

What benefits did God promise to the obedient in Deuteronomy 4:5-8?

Psalm 89:15 and Isaiah 30:18 very specifically include happiness among the blessings God delivers. Think beyond cars and condos. In what ways have you seen God's justice carried out against "evildoers"?

In what ways have you seen happiness showered on obedient believers?

Based on the word "delight" in Malachi 3:1, "it appears that Israel had repeated the error of their forebears in the days of Amos (Amos 5:18) by supposing that the Lord's appearance would be unmitigated good news. When he comes, it will be not only for blessing, as they assume, but also for judgment."[4]

Why do you think we tend to be more critical of the plank in other people's eyes when it's the same variety of wood clouding our own spiritual vision? (See Matt. 7:1-5.)

scene four

IMPLICATION (TO ISRAEL):

Behold, I send my messenger, and he will prepare the way before me … says the LORD of hosts. Malachi 3:1

Because of the seriousness of the charge of injustice the Israelites levied against Him, God takes the megaphone back from Malachi to make a personal response. Yet instead of justifiably wiping His rebellious, self-indulgent children off the map, He leans down, gently puts His hands on either side of their face, and lovingly reminds them of His merciful plan for their future.

First He tells them that John the Baptist (remember Jesus' cousin, the one who wore a roadkill coat and had grasshopper legs stuck in his teeth?), His "messenger," is coming. Then God's grin widens before He tells them the best part: that Jesus—the Messiah they've been waiting on for what seems like forever, the "messenger of the covenant"—will be hot on Johnny B's heels!

I can't help but think of Jesus' parable about 10 girls who were waiting on a husband (see Matt. 25:1-13). Five of these brides-to-be were wise and brought extra oil to keep their lamps burning while they waited. Five of them were flighty and didn't think to bring extra oil. Their lamps went out. Then, while they were off getting more oil at Home Depot, the bridegroom comes and they miss him, leaving them forever stranded at the altar.

By reminding His people that the Messiah's entrance was imminent, God effectively poured more oil into their flickering lamps. Instead of giving them a spanking, He gave them hope. He guaranteed them their puffy white dress wasn't going to have to stay in the closet sealed in plastic because their Bridegroom. Really. Was. Coming.

What does a never-worn, plastic-wrapped wedding dress symbolize for you? In other words, what have you asked God for that seems to be taking forever to happen?

How can you turn God's promise to the grumbling people of Malachi's day into a source of encouragement for your own waiting heart?

In the Old Testament, the word *covenant*—*berit* in Hebrew— "entails four essential components: (1) a relationship (2) with a nonrelative that (3) involves obligations and (4) is established through an oath. It is used seven times in Malachi (out of a mere 1,193 words): a rate 10 times greater than almost every other OT book (except for Deuteronomy, Joshua, Hosea, and Obadiah). This may explain why Malachi goes out of his way to identify marriage as a "covenant" (Proverbs is the only other book to do so explicitly). Malachi is also the only book to use the designation, "the messenger [or angel] of the covenant."[5]

After assuring them of the advent of the Messiah, God gives His people a little dissertation on discipline. He explains that instead of the justice they're demanding—which of course would mean them getting zapped right alongside the "eva-durs" they'd jabbed their fingers at—He was going to *refine* them. And while pastors often recite Malachi 3:2-4 in deep, menacing James Earl Jones tones (when I was little and Brother Boyington got to this part in his sermon series on the Minor Prophets, it vibrated the whole pew), I think God's voice was actually tinged with more tenderness than fury because He compares His kids to gold and silver, *precious* metals still valuable in today's economy.

God continues the implication by explaining that His refining process is restorative, that divine discipline will purify their lives and make them more beautiful, but that it was going to sting. A lot. Because a refiner's fire has to be hot enough to separate the dross from molten metal—gold melts at approximately 1,337 degrees Fahrenheit. Because in Old Testament times a fuller used strong lye soap to separate stubborn dirt and grease from clothes, then laid the laundry on a rock, beat it with a stick, and scrubbed it with a stiff brush until it was clean again.

The bottom line is that true repentance never comes cheaply, but the intimacy it affords us with our Redeemer is invaluable.

Think of the most painful refining you've yet gone through. From your present perspective, was the result worth the pain? Why or why not?

Have you ever earnestly prayed for Jesus to "hurry up and come back" because you didn't feel like you could stand your life one minute longer? If so, explain.

Does reading 2 Peter 3:8-9 right now help you hang onto hope or does it mostly annoy you? Honesty is OK here.

The Lord of hosts closes out His commentary with a list of seven sins He will judge swiftly on the day of his coming: sorcery; adultery; swearing dishonestly in His name; cheating on the pay of hired workers; oppression of widows and orphans; mistreating sojourners and aliens; and not fearing and not respecting Him.

    The passage makes me want to steer clear of Ouija boards, desperate housewives, stingy employers, and politicians who say ugly things about people!

How was Simeon's encounter in Luke 2:25-35 a partial fulfillment of the prophecy in Malachi 3:1?

How would you explain Jeremiah 32:39 to a child?

In light of Proverbs 3:11-12 and Hebrews 12:3-11, how has God showed His love for you recently?

The "day of his coming" ("day of the Lord" in other translations) in the fourth disputation, has as its goal the "purification" of God's people "as a whole," not merely a portion. "Thus 'Judah and Jerusalem,' capital and country, function together to suggest the completeness of the sanctification of God's people. From the point of view of biblical hermeneutics, any subsequent people of God—including Christians in the current covenant age—can be the referent (Gal. 3:29)."[6]

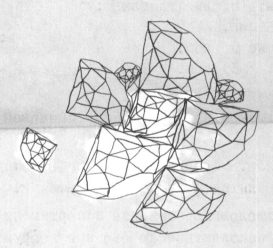

MINING PERSONAL JEWELS FROM MALACHI'S STORY

Look up the history of the song, "Swing Low, Sweet Chariot" and listen to at least one version (several versions are available on iTunes and Google).

Sing a Song

1. **After** singing "Swing Low, Sweet Chariot" through several times to yourself, rewrite the lyrics in your own "dialect."

2. **Bring** your revision of this classic "call and response chant" to Bible study next week.

3. **Sing it**—or at least recite it!— to your small group.

6. God's miraculous return on our meager investments

Sabrina, Krystal, and Sheri are three of the recovering heroes I've gotten to walk with for six months at The Next Door, and we've forged a bond like the four Musketeers. I love Sabrina's big grin, her palpable compassion for others who suffer, and the way she always prays, "Dear Lord, thank you for loving me when I couldn't love myself" when ending our sessions. I love Krystal's dry sense of humor and the way she makes her eyes bug out when she's acting out the feeling of "surprise" while telling a story. And I love Sheri's gentle spirit and the way her whole face lights up when she talks about her children.

Not only have I fallen in love with their personalities, I also deeply respect the way this trio wrestles the beast of addiction so courageously. In fact, I don't know a group of women I admire more—which I proclaim repeatedly and with such enthusiasm that sometimes even dark brown Sabrina blushes! But I know the flush of verbal encouragement tends to wear off quickly, so I bring a tiny bit of tangible encouragement on Wednesday nights too. I always bring chocolate (which is admittedly self-serving), as well as an amenity they don't have easy access to in a half-way house environment—something like yummy-smelling Aveda shampoo, new socks, or urban Christian music CDs. Just a little reminder that someone is pulling for them while they're fighting the toughest battle of their lives.

So when I got to travel to Ireland this past June, I made sure to pick up a few souvenirs for my three Next Door friends too. I bought some fancy European chocolate that I've never seen before in the States, three miniature Celtic crosses, three "I ♥ Ireland" bumper stickers, and three very cheesy leprechaun key chains. I was also mindful about keeping a few coins when I exchanged my leftover European currency back into dollars at the Dublin airport, assuming Sabrina, Krystal, and Sheri might enjoy seeing the difference between their money and our money.

But when I returned home to Tennessee and was getting ready to see the girls again, I thought twice about bringing them the Euros. I wondered if giving them foreign coins would come across as condescending since that's the kind of memento you typically give a child. The last thing I want to do is behave in a way that comes across as belittling to these women I respect so much. After thinking about it for awhile, I reasoned that because none of them have had the privilege of traveling outside the country yet they might think the Euros were interesting, so I left them in my Bible study bag.

Of course the girls were sweet and appreciative as usual about the tchotchkes—they ate the chocolate, put the stickers on their Bible study notebooks, told me they were going to hang the crosses in their rooms, pretended they would use the key chains when they got their driver's licenses back, and then split the Euros among themselves, proclaiming the coins to be "cool." Then, as is our normal routine, we put the treats aside after a few minutes to tell each other about our weeks and ponder a story about Jesus together. I didn't give the Irish booty another thought until I got home later that night and realized my phone was buzzing with a text from Sheri. This is the exact wording:

SHERI:

i promise i'm not harassing you lol, but one quick story: one of the worst things i did, that i feel the worst about was when i stole my dads extremely cool and rare coin collection so i could get high. But with no gift for fathers day yet i now have the best gift i could have gave him, a new rare and cool coin! That's how Jesus works! thanks lisa

When I went back to visit her the next day, Sheri explained the details of the story. How the lowest point in her addiction had come about a year earlier when she stole her dad's coin collection and pawned it so she could use the money for more drugs. She said she felt especially ashamed of taking what had been important to her father because he was her biggest supporter. Unlike most everyone else in her life, he'd never given up on her. Not when she got arrested for a third DUI while her baby was in the car with her; not when she went to jail; not even when she was forced to give up custody of her children temporarily because of her oxycodone habit. She said, "That's why out of all the people I could've stolen from, I really hate that I stole from my *dad."*

She went on to describe how she'd been worried about what, if anything, she could get him for Father's Day this year because after paying her fees at The Next Door and sending her mom cash to help take care of her kids, she didn't have much money leftover. Then she beamed at me and said, "But then you showed up and gave me that rare and precious coin which is the *perfect* Father's Day gift. I can't wait to give it to him on Sunday!" (This took place on the Thursday before Father's Day.)

I wasn't able to say much in response to Sheri, because by then I had tears streaming down my face and I didn't want to collapse into a heap of uncontrollable blubbering like I'd done with Eva. So I just handed her a velvet bag containing every foreign coin I'd been able to dig out of my closet, after receiving her text the night before, and said, "Why don't you give him these too?"

I am continually amazed by how generous our Redeemer is to His beloved. How He woos us with fragrant flowers and peachy sunsets and dear friendships. How He winks at us before putting the big corner brownie—the one with two sides of crunchy chocolate goodness—on our plate. How He gallantly covers our shameful mistakes with the cape of His mercy. And how the tiniest investment of worship on our end unleashes an avalanche of blessing from His! God's lavish mercy is the essence of this next message in Malachi.

video notes:

_____

_____

_____

_____

_____

_____

_____

_____

_____

_____

hosea: salvation

malachi: messenger

metonym: true story

God will never abandon His beloved.

1. If you had a Hosea in your life how would it impact you?

2. Is there a Hosea in your life who didn't leave or abandon you when you deserved to be left? If so, how has their undeserved faithfulness affected you?

3. How does the story of Hosea and Gomer show you a new perspective on the gospel story of Jesus' unconditional, unchanging love?

"Grace means you're in a different universe from where you had been stuck, when you had absolutely no way to get there on your own."

—ANNE LAMOTT[2]

1. Merriam-Webster's Collegiate® Dictionary, 10th ed. (Springfield, MA: Merriam-Webster, Inc, 1997), 782.
2. Anne Lamott, *Plan B* (New York: Riverhead Books, 2005), 54–55.
Video downloads and additional leader helps available at lifeway.com/lisaharper

scene 1
assertion (from God): Malachi 3:6-7a

scene 2
questioning (by Israel): Malachi 3:7b

scene 3
assertion (from God): Malachi 3:8a

scene 4
questioning (from Israel): Malachi 3:8b

scene 5
response (from God): Malachi 3:8c
implication (from God): Malachi 3:9-12

how can I give God more of me?

SETTING THE STAGE

I went to a small school in southeast Alabama called Troy University for my last two years of undergrad, and my favorite professor on campus was Dean Merrill Bankester (who is now Dean Emeritus of the Hall School of Journalism and Communication at Troy). He was kind and funny and always seemed genuinely interested in his students. He's the first professor most of my friends and I went to if we were having problems in our other classes, if we needed a recommendation for a job, or if we just wanted someone wise to bounce ideas off of regarding what we wanted to do for the rest of our lives.

Did you have a favorite teacher or professor? What made this person so likeable?

I liked Dean Bankester so much that I signed up for every class he taught. The only problem was, most of his seminars were early in the morning and I was a social butterfly (aka: night owl) in college. Which meant I typically had a hard time staying awake in his classes. And while I did everything I could to stay upright and alert—I sipped Diet Coke, I bit the inside of my lip, I shifted sitting positions, I pressed my fingernails into my palms—it was almost always a losing battle because the longer Dean Bankester lectured, the heavier my eyelids got until I just couldn't keep them open any more. I invariably ended up slumped in my seat, eyes closed, and mouth wide open like an old man in a recliner on Thanksgiving afternoon.

As gracious as Dean Bankester was, he eventually got tired of my narcoleptic routine. So one morning at the beginning of my senior year, he decided to teach me a lesson. He waited until I was unconscious and then made this announcement (which was repeated to me after the fact): "Ladies and gentlemen, I'm going to dismiss class early today. However, since Ms. Harper is sleeping peacefully I'd appreciate it if you'd exit the room quietly so as not to disturb her." Of course the snickering started immediately, quickly followed by the sound of dozens of desk legs scraping against the wooden floor, which woke me up from my nap. I was dazed and confused for a few seconds before it occurred to me that Dean Bankester had singled me out for my untimely snoring!

Describe a time you've been called out, maybe even embarrassed by your actions. What happened as a result?

In the second disputation (see Mal. 1:6–2:9), God singled out the Israelite priests for dishonoring Him with their puny scratch-and-dent offerings. But now the whole class is getting called on the carpet for chintzy offerings. His divine spotlight revealed that *all* of Israel was guilty of halfhearted worship.

INTRODUCING NEW CHARACTERS

The fifth disputation begins with a reference to characters who aren't technically new—just *newly named* since this is the first time in Malachi that God refers to the Israelites as the "children of Jacob" (Mal. 3:6). Which is basically just Yahweh's way of flipping through the pages of the Hebrew family album to remind His people about how worship has been an ongoing issue throughout their history. Because when Jacob (Abraham's second-born twin grandson—"Heely" from Mal. 2) returned to the promised land from *his exile* in Paddan-aram (Gen. 28:1-5), he'd built an altar and made a solemn vow to give God $\frac{1}{10}$ of his income.

Read Genesis 28:20-22. What motivated Jacob to make this vow to love God forever and give Him $\frac{1}{10}$ of what he owned?

In what circumstances have you promised to love God forever and give Him at least of portion of everything you own?

Likewise, when the Israelites returned from *their exile* in Babylon, they rebuilt the altar in Jerusalem—unfortunately they were grossly neglecting the vow their great-great-great and then some granddaddy Jacob made.

The events in the Book of Nehemiah took place during the same period as the Book of Malachi. Nehemiah restored the temple worship, but the people weren't bringing their offerings, so the Levite priests were forced to find another way to make a living (see Neh. 13:10). You can compare the Levites in Nehemiah's story to our church staffs today. If all church members stop tithing, or significantly reduce their tithe, some salaries couldn't be paid. And if some salaries couldn't be paid then some of the church staff would be forced to find other employment, which could have a very negative effect on corporate worship.

What do you think tithing should look like for Christians who've lost their jobs and are struggling financially?

Nehemiah corrected the problem of his day, " 'Why is the house of God forsaken?' And I gathered them together and set them in their stations. Then all Judah brought the tithe of the grain, wine, and oil into the storehouses" (13:11-12).

As was the case in Nehemiah, Malachi's peers needed a stern reminder about fulfilling the vow their forefather Jacob made. Which reminds me of my 11th grade anatomy teacher, Mrs. Cabal. When I asked to be excused to go to the restroom the first time I came face to muzzle with the dead cat we were about to dissect, she remarked, "I can't believe you're Theresa Harper's sister because she wasn't squeamish at all!"

Bringing up my sister's stoicism with stiff kitties was her way of telling me to "Buck up" and uphold the academic standards my sister had established, which I think was pretty much what God was doing when He reminded the Israelites of their blood ties to Jacob.

scene one

ASSERTION (FROM GOD):

For I the LORD do not change; therefore you, O children of Jacob, are not consumed. From the days of your fathers you have turned aside from my statutes and have not kept them. Return to me, and I will return to you, says the LORD of hosts. Malachi 3:6-7a

Recall Jacob's vow to God in Genesis 28:20-22. Why do you think God addresses them as "children of Jacob"?

While on the surface these passages in Genesis and Malachi may only seem to address tithing, the deeper issue is that God desired an intimate relationship with them. "O children of Jacob" isn't just a reminder of their lineage, it also expresses God's deep love for His people.

Pause and reflect on the fact that God desires relationship with His people. And why is "giving" such an important aspect of our relationship with Him?

I went out and got two Jack Russell terrier puppies the day after Reba died; Harley—a shy, rather effeminate boy dog—and Dottie—his bossy sister, built like a miniature Walrus with a fat body

how are you like these Jack Russell terriers?

list the good ways along with the bad. and no, we're not looking for comparisons like Dottie's waddle here. Think in terms of our devotion to and ways we run away from God.

and very short legs. Those two stinkers have provided me with so much joy over the past eight years. They run to the gate (well, actually Dottie does more of a fast waddle), sausage tails wagging wildly, whenever they hear my car coming up the driveway. And they run/waddle to the top of the highest hill in the front yard whenever they hear me backing out of the driveway, like two wee friends waving me off from the dock as I sail away on errands! They climb all over me if I'm ever silly enough to lie down in their vicinity; and they vigorously defend our small homestead whenever the UPS man, the pest control guy, or even a bizarrely anxious woman threatens the perimeter.

They are also determined escape artists who spend at least half of their waking hours plotting how to dig under the fence or dart out of a gate carelessly left open. Their goal—their "holy grail" if you will—is the thousands of acres of undeveloped federal land chock full of squirrels, rabbits, deer, raccoons, foxes, and wild turkeys that just happens to butt up to the back of my property. You can almost see the passionate longing beating in their squatty dog hearts when they stand at the fence, staring at that fringe of forbidden wilderness, only 50 yards from the back door.

As is the hallmark of little dogs, they usually manage to get what they want. So every month or two I can be heard clomping through the woods for hours calling out, "Doottiiee, Haarrlleeyy … Come heeeerree … I have a *treat* for you!" It's not that I don't want them to enjoy the freedom of racing through fields and forests and terrorizing a varmint or two, it's just that there are so many life-threatening hazards out there and I don't want either of them to get hurt. I can't help breathing a happy sigh of relief when those pudgy pups are safely back home, in spite of the fact that their fur is tangled with burrs and their bellies are speckled with ticks.

Our Heavenly Father's commitment to His headstrong children's well-being is infinitely stronger than my devotion to a pair of stubborn dogs. Which is why He beckons them to *return home* to Him.

scene two

QUESTIONING (BY ISRAEL):

But you say, "How shall we return?"

Malachi 3:7b

Harley was always the first one to return from their jaunts into the great beyond. Usually within minutes of coming home empty-handed after searching for them for hours—after traipsing up and down hills, cutting my arms and legs all to pieces on briars, and trashing yet another pair of running shoes with mud and gunk—I'd hear his toenails clicking softly on the back porch. And when I threw the door open, he'd be sitting there with his ears cocked and head tilted to one side as if to say, "Where have *you* been? I've been sitting here forever, just twirling my paws and waiting for you to come outside!"

Six weeks ago I had to have Harley put down because he had advanced lymphoma. It just about killed me to stroke his sleepy face, look into his trusting golden eyes, and tell him what a good boy he was while Dr. Edwards gave him the shot that I knew would cause his brave little heart to stop pumping for good. I still miss him. Several times since he's been gone I've found myself opening the back door and half hoping to find him sitting there again, looking up at me with that comically puzzled expression I'd seen him wear so many times before.

I don't know if the Israelites were feigning innocence again when they questioned God's command to return to Him or if they were genuinely puzzled about how to do so. This question could also have been their way of communicating pessimism, the way teenagers today ask, *"Really?"* with one eyebrow cocked and voices dripping with sarcasm.

Regardless of the motive behind why the Israelites asked, "How?" they definitely needed a nudge from God to begin their journey back home. They remind me of 2 Samuel 12:1-13, where it took a friend basically shaking David by the shoulders for him to see his own sin.

Have you ever been like David, where you needed a good jolt to see your responsibility honestly? If so, describe the situation.

When is the last time you heard yourself ask God, *How?* when you sensed Him commanding you to do something difficult?

Old Testament scholars have disagreed regarding whether the fifth disputation of Malachi begins in 3:6 or 3:7. However, since the fourth disputation ends naturally and logically with a summarizing statement and a messenger formula ("says the LORD of hosts"), there seems to be more of a consensus that it begins with 3:6.

scene three

ASSERTION (FROM GOD): Will man rob God?

Yet you are robbing me. Malachi 3:8a

When John Price was 2 or 3 years old, he became very enamored with the hat pins displayed on the counter of the B&W, our neighborhood convenience store. It didn't matter to him that he didn't have a hat to affix them to, he was still totally enchanted by those shiny, dime-sized discs featuring rebel flags, beer cans, football team mascots, and female silhouettes. So whenever Mom took him inside the store with her to buy a gallon of milk or a loaf of bread, he surreptitiously helped himself to some. Mom didn't discover his stash until he'd amassed enough hat pins to cover a sombrero. Of course, she was mortified and piled us into the car for an ominously quiet drive to the B&W.

When we got there, Mom marched John inside to confess his sin. I hung back by the potato chip rack stifling a giggle because he wasn't tall enough to see over the counter, which forced Mom to reach down and lift J.P. up onto the surface in order for him to face the store manager, Mrs. Wiggins, an elderly woman who I thought was scary because she rarely smiled, had a towering beehive hairdo, and had been known to chase gum-stealing kids off the premises with a broom. After John admitted to swiping her wares, she exclaimed indignantly, "I can't believe he stole them. After all, he's just a baby!" Mrs. Wiggins couldn't believe that a tow-headed toddler barely out of Pampers was foolhardy enough to shoplift from her store.

Did you ever get caught taking something that wasn't yours? If so, describe the incident including how you felt when you got caught.

Dumb and Dumber is how you can describe the Israelite's scheme to pilfer stuff from *God's* store. After all, He's the one who breathed our universe into existence, who hung the stars in place, and who tells the sun where to hide 'til morning, and they were mere *humans!*

Read Psalm 139:1-12. Under what circumstances does this passage make you feel more secure?

Under what circumstances does it make you feel more anxious?

The Hebrew word used in the fifth disputation of Malachi for "tithe" is **maʿăśēr** (3:8), which means "setting aside a tenth,"[1] while the Hebrew word used in this disputation for "offering" is **tĕrûmâ** (3:8), which means "offering, special gift, contribution."[2] In light of the dozens of uses of **tĕrûmâ** throughout the Old Testament to refer to all sorts of offerings, and in the absence of any contextual indication to the contrary, it seems likely that "offerings in general" is what **tĕrûmâ** means in Malachi 3 and that **maʿăśēr** means more specifically the obligation to give 1/10 one's income to Yahweh annually.[3]

scene four

QUESTIONING (FROM ISRAEL):

But you say, "How have we robbed you?"

Malachi 3:8b

Hmm, let me see. Maybe when you folded a single $20 bill over a roll of ones and assumed God didn't notice? Or when you put a *People* magazine between the pages of your Bible and pretended you were studying His Word when in actuality you were gazing at celebrity gossip? Or when you faked spiritual devotion on the outside but were really just a big, fat Pharisee on the inside? Speaking of Pharisees, this is how Jesus called them on the carpet when they tried to camouflage their thieving hearts like their forefathers—the Israelites—had done in Malachi.

Read Matthew 23:25-28. How does God view our outward actions and our inward feelings?

The overarching good news in this fifth disputation is we can't outgive God; the bad news is we can't hide our crooked hearts from Him either.

Read Mark 12:41-44. What's your favorite modern-day "widow's mite" story?

scene five

RESPONSE (FROM GOD):

In your tithes and contributions.

Malachi 3:8c

In the pilot episode of *The Cosby Show* (my all-time favorite family sitcom), Dr. Cliff Huxtable (Bill Cosby) has a discussion with his 14-year-old son, Theo (Malcolm-Jamal Warner), regarding the "D's" on his report card. Theo tries to reason with his dad that his grades really don't matter, since he's just going to be a "regular" person when he grows up, at which Dr. Huxtable becomes hilariously exasperated. Their conversation went something like this.

THEO:

"You're a doctor and Mom's a lawyer, and you're both successful in everything and that's great! But maybe I was born to be a regular person and have a regular life. If you weren't a doctor, I wouldn't love you less, because you're my dad. So rather than feeling disappointed because I'm not like you, maybe you should accept who I am and love me anyway, because I'm your son."

CLIFF:

"Theo … that's the dumbest thing I've ever heard in my life! No wonder you get D's in everything! You're afraid to try because you're afraid your brain is going to ex-

Shicheth (pronounced shih KHAYT) is a Hebrew word that means *destroy, corrupt,* or *ruined.* It's used three times in the Book of Malachi: 1:14 when God accuses the Israelite priests of sacrificing defective animals; 2:8 when God declares the Israelite priests have violated the covenant of Levi; and in 3:11 when God talks about the ruination of produce in the land of Israel.[4]

plode and it's going to ooze out of your ears. Now I'm telling you, you are going to try as hard as you can. And you're going to do it because I said so. I am your father. I brought you into this world, and I'll take you out!"[5]

I love Dr. Cliff's line: "I brought you into this world, and I'll take you out!" I think it's one of the funniest things I've ever heard a television parent say to a disobedient kid and it's definitely what I would have said to the Israelites if I'd been their mama! But instead of threatening annihilation, our supernaturally patient Heavenly Father clarifies His message to His children for the bazillionth time.

Compare Exodus 19:5; Leviticus 20:26; and Psalm 50:10. How would you describe the difference between offerings *given by* their owners with offerings *given to* their owner?

If you had to rate the cheerfulness of your heart on a scale of 1 to 10, with 1 being *resentful,* 5 being *resigned,* 10 being *rejoicing,* when you write a check for church and/or ministry, where would you be on the scale?

1 | resentful

rejoicing | 10

OFFERINGS GIVEN BY	OFFERINGS GIVEN TO

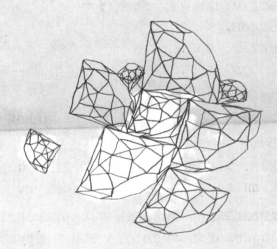

MINING JEWELS FROM MALACHI'S STORY

Write your regular tithe check (or write the amount of what you're giving through direct deposit on a piece of paper) sometime this week before going to church. Do this task in a private place where there's plenty of room.

Make a Joyful Noise

1. Write the check (or the number symbolizing what you're giving).

2. Make a joyful physical "noise"—do a cartwheel, do the Macarena, do the two-step, or just wiggle something in order to practice being a cheerful giver!

7. the promise of pirouetting livestock

Joseph Carey Merrick (often incorrectly referred to as "John") was a man who lived in 19th-century England. Because of his extreme disfigurement, he was maliciously called "The Elephant Man" (also the title of a 1980 movie about his life). Joseph was born with a rare disorder called *neurofibromatosis*, which causes the growth of noncancerous tumors on nerve tissue, producing skin and bone abnormalities. His mother died when he was 11, and Joseph was forced to fend for himself after his father and stepmother rejected him. He made an arrangement with an abusive factory owner who—like the wicked stepmother in Cinderella—forced him to work for his keep.

A carnival showman discovered Joseph when he was 14 and decided he could make money by exploiting Joseph's deformities. Fortunately, the carnival stopped in London for a performance and set up across the street from a hospital. When Dr. Frederick Treves saw a crude drawing of Joseph advertising him as "The Elephant Man" he was intrigued and paid a shilling to see him. This is Dr. Treves' description of what he saw.

DR. TREVES: ... a bony mass protruding from his brow; spongy skin, with a fissured surface resembling brown cauliflower hanging in folds from his back; a huge, misshapen head the circumference of a man's waist; the mouth a distorted, slobbering aperture; the nose a dangling lump of skin; a bag of flesh like the dewlap of a lizard suspended from the chest. His

right arm was overgrown to twice its normal
size, its fingers stubby and useless. Flaps
of skin in the shape of a paddle descended
from one armpit; deformed legs supported
him only if he held onto a chair. A sicken-
ing stench emanated from the fungous skin
growths.[1]

After viewing Joseph Merrick, Dr. Treves wanted to document his medical condition so he arranged to have him examined at the hospital. They performed tests, took photographs, and tried to communicate with Joseph, but because of his misshapen mouth he couldn't speak clearly and no one could understand him. Nor were they aware of the inhumane conditions he was forced to live in. At the end of the examination, Dr. Treves put his card in Joseph's coat pocket and walked him back across the street to the carnival, not knowing that it was leaving town the next day.

Two years later the carnival closed down for good. The unscrupulous manager stole all of Joseph's earnings and roughly shoved him on a train back to London. Although Joseph wore a cloak and a veil, he was beaten by other passengers because of his frightening appearance. He had to be rescued by policemen as soon as the train arrived at the London terminal. While trying to discern his identity, the police found the soiled card of Dr. Treves in Joseph's coat and called him. Dr. Treves, who'd thought of Joseph many times since their brief encounter but didn't know how to find him again, hurried to the police station and carefully escorted him back to the hospital.

It was during his second, lengthy stay at the hospital that Dr. Treves discovered rather than being an imbecile, Joseph was actually a very intelligent man with a beautiful spirit. Treves recorded his observations in a diary.

DR. TREVES: His troubles had ennobled him. He showed himself to be a gentle, affectionate and lovable creature … without a grievance and without an unkind word for anyone. I have never heard him complain. I have never heard him deplore his ruined life or resent the treatment he had received at the hands of callous keepers. His journey through life had been indeed along a *via dolorosa,* the road had been uphill all the way.[2]

Most of the people (including Alexandra, Princess of Wales) who were fortunate enough to meet Joseph Carey Merrick during the last few years of his life were amazed by his gracious disposition because it defied the laws of behavioral science. In light of the horrifically abusive treatment he'd received since childhood, he should have grown into an adult with the temperament of a rabid animal. Instead the phrase he repeated most often before dying in his sleep of asphyxiation at the age of 28 was, "I am happy every hour of the day."

When you compare Joseph's compassionate nature with the factory owner, the carnival manager, and the bullies on the train who were so cruel to him during his short life, it's like the epitome of good and evil. All of God's children may be created equally, but we don't all turn out the same. Some, like Joseph, grow up to have beautiful hearts that resemble their Heavenly Father, while some grow up to have twisted, ugly, self-centered spirits that don't resemble their divine Dad at all. This is the downside of the sixth and final disputation in Malachi; the upside is that God's good kids get to boogie like baby cows set free from a claustrophobic stall!

video notes:

_____

_____

_____

_____

_____

_____

_____

_____

_____

_____

_____

_____

God never lets His people go.

For more information on The Next Door, please visit *www.thenextdoor.org*

1. How do you relate to
   Sabrina's prayer,
   "God thank you for
   loving me even when I
   couldn't love myself"?
   What else about Sa-
   brina's story could
   you relate to?

2. How has God shown you
   He loved you, no mat-
   ter how mistake-prone
   you are?

3. Describe a time you
   felt forgotten but God
   saw you. How does it
   feel to be found?

"In God's story, you are the focus
of a celebration. Not what you've done.
You. ... In your story you are
going to continue searching for
a reason God should love you.
In your story you are going to
continue finding reasons he shouldn't.
So here's my suggestion:
give up your version of your story
and embrace his."

—ANDY STANLEY

Andy Stanley, *The Grace of God* (Nashville, TN: Thomas Nelson, 2010), 216.

Video downloads and additional leader helps available at lifeway.com/lisaharper

scene 1
assertion (from God): Malachi 3:13a

scene 2
questioning (from Israel): Malachi 3:13b

scene 3
response (from God): Malachi 3:14-15

scene 4
implication (from God): Malachi 3:16-4:6

how does the second coming of Christ
influence my daily perspective?

SETTING THE STAGE

When I was at Troy, I joined a sorority. I know there are some negative stereotypes about fraternities and sororities—of spoiled coeds skipping classes, clandestine meetings with cultish themes, and drunken toga parties—but that wasn't my experience. The Greek system in small-town Alabama was more *Little House on the Prairie* than *Animal House.*

I didn't like one aspect of sorority life though, and that was the element of exclusivity. I didn't like the way some girls were picked to be on a particular sorority "team," while other girls weren't. I remember one meeting when all of us Kappa Deltas were gathered together in a big circle discussing which girls we thought were a fit for our sorority and which girls weren't. The conversation was pleasant at first until one of the haughty older "sisters" began vehemently blackballing some possible pledges because of their mediocre grades, their less-than-stellar looks, or their parents' menial jobs. She even made fun of one girl's size and declared her "too fat" to be a Kappa Delta.

I was mad as a wet hen—I've never really understood that colloquialism, perhaps because I've never squirted a hose at a chicken before, but I like it—and I let her know it. I stood up in the circle and made an impassioned plea about how we shouldn't stoop to that kind of pretentious selectivity. After several of my friends applauded and nodded their heads affirmatively, my monologue became more fervent and I declared that if she was going to be that picky, she needed to just start her own snooty sorority because we would Not. Turn. One. Single. Girl. Away.

A little while later, after I excused myself to sweeten my iced tea in the kitchen and secretly gloat for a minute, one of the selection committee members wandered in and said sheepishly, "Hey Lisa, we might need you to come back into the meeting and amend what you proposed about us not turning anyone away." I gave her a perplexed look and asked indignantly, "What do you mean?" She answered logically, if not a little apologetically, "Well, one girl who requested to join Kappa Delta has been arrested for writing bad checks and another was just picked up by campus police while climbing out a bedroom window at the Sigma Chi house stark naked in the middle of the day!"

Although selection processes go against my grain, I've had to come to terms with the fact that sometimes winnowing is needed. In Malachi's case, the line was absolutely necessary between those who were *for* God and those who were *against* Him.

If you were God, setting the admission standards for His kingdom, do you think you'd be harsher or gentler than He is? Why?

Describe a time when you have been excluded. How did it feel, and why was it fair or unfair?

INTRODUCING NEW CHARACTERS

When I joined Sabrina and some of her friends from "The Freedom Recovery Center" on Thanksgiving Day to pass out food to the homeless, my favorite part was driving all over town in my car praying about which person God had chosen for us to give the next plate to. About 30 minutes into our mission, while in a very sketchy part of downtown Nashville, I spotted a guy who certainly looked starved. He was tall and skinny, wearing dirty jeans pulled down low over his hips, and was weaving noticeably on the sidewalk, which I took to mean that he was faint with hunger. Since he had his back to us, I wasn't sure how old he was, but I was positive he needed our help. So I poked Sabrina in the arm as she sat in the passenger seat and squealed, "Hey Sabrina, *there's* somebody!" while screeching to a stop behind him.

Sabrina shot me a bemused look and said, "Lisa, he ain't hungry. Look at his *shoes.*" When I looked down, I was surprised to see he was wearing really expensive Nikes, however by then it was too late because my intended meal target had already spun around with an angry expression—probably mad that I'd almost run him over on a holiday! But the second he saw Sabrina, his expression shifted from I'm-about-to-mess-you-up-lady to astonishment. He lifted his hand slightly in a guarded greeting and said, "Hey Sabrina." She nodded back and said, "Hey Jermaine. How you doin'?" He mumbled something I couldn't understand and she handed him a bag of food, gave him a sort of side hug, and said kindly, "See ya" before getting back in the car.

When she rolled her window up, I said, "Wow, you *know* that guy?" She turned toward me with an embarrassed grin and a shrug of her shoulders, "Yeah. He used to be my dealer." I stared at her for a few seconds, at this beautiful, compassionate woman who radiates the love of Jesus. It's difficult for me to imagine her lost in a sea of alcohol and drugs and yet she was for over 20 years. She is one of God's *reclaimed* treasures.

Can you think of a time when, like me, you misjudged someone terribly? If so, tell me about it.

Like Sabrina, the new characters in this last passage of Malachi have been restored by our Redeemer's amazing grace. Through His leading, they have decisively turned away from evil and turned toward what God calls "good." They are the ones our Heavenly Father calls His treasured possessions.

God is the dominant speaker in the first, second, fifth, and sixth disputations. "Only the 'center disputations,' the third and the fourth, are characterized by a predominance of prophetic speech" wherein God is *spoken about* rather than *speaking Himself*.[3]

scene one

ASSERTION (FROM GOD):

Your words have been hard against me, says the LORD. Malachi 3:13a

When I was first learning how to use the integrated Bluetooth phone system in my car, I was like a squirrel on a unicycle—totally inept and out of my element. First of all, the whole thing seemed to have a mind of its own. I'd be cruising down the interstate, happily howling like the James Taylor background singer I think I was born to be, when suddenly I'd hear a faint voice in the distance saying, "Hello? Hello? Lisa?" And before I had time to figure out how to mute the music—which according to the manual that came with the car was supposed to happen automatically—the voice would get louder in pitch and accusatory in tone, "Lisa? LISA? IS THAT YOU? TURN DOWN THE MUSIC SO I CAN HEAR YOU!"

But being jolted out of James Taylor nirvana was mild compared to what happened a year and a half ago when the Bluetooth demon in my car redialed perky Hilda Hoohah (names have been changed to protect the innocent) immediately after we'd hung up and *while* I was gossiping about how her bouncy personality got on my nerves to another friend who was running errands with me. Of course, there were no flashing red lights or ominous GPS voice warning, "Stop talking immediately, Lisa, because your now wounded friend Hilda can hear every unkind word you're saying." Oh no, that kind of technology would have been helpful so it wasn't included in the sticker price! The only hint I had regarding her unfortunate eavesdropping was the distinct disconnecting noise that's made when whoever you've been talking to hangs up their phone, followed by the words "Call with Hilda Hoohah ended" on the dashboard screen.

Help me out here! Please tell me I'm not alone in having a horribly embarrassing gossipy moment like the one I just described. What's your story of a conversation-gone-wrong moment you'd like a do-over on?

The minutes between realizing my catty chatter had been broadcast and calling Hilda on a landline to apologize ticked off slower than time spent in a Jenny Craig lobby waiting to be weighed in. I had spoken harsh words against her and she had overheard every single one. Such was the situation at the beginning of the last argument Malachi records between the Israelites and Yahweh.

What does Jesus' teaching in Matthew 12:33-37 say about the harsh words we, and the people in Malachi's experience, utter?

If you were teaching Ephesians 4:29 and Romans 14:19 to a children's Sunday School class, what story would you tell to drive the point home?

Does Proverbs 10:19 comfort you or convict you? Explain your answer.

scene two

QUESTIONING (FROM ISRAEL):

But you say, "How have we spoken against
you?" Malachi 3:13b

I've never been in a beauty pageant but I went to college with lots of girls who were because in Alabama, pageants are a rite of passage for lots of young women. That may be why the Deep South has more baton-twirling tutors per capita than anywhere else in the country. One of my sorority sisters was Miss Rattlesnake Roundup and another was the Peanut Festival Queen. But I didn't meet a real Miss America until I graduated from college.

It all started a few months after graduation when I ran into a girl I knew from middle school (who will from now on be referred to as "Smiley" to ward off any future lawsuits). Smiley and I hadn't seen each other in years so we gabbed and caught up. I told her about the youth ministry I was working for, and she told me that she'd recently won a state beauty pageant title and was soon to compete in the Miss America pageant. When I congratulated her, she winked and asked me to pray for her because she thought she had a good chance of winning.

Several months later my friend Emily asked me to go to a women's expo with her at the convention center in Birmingham. It was comprised of several hundred booths promoting specialty items, so thousands of women were roaming up and down the aisles gawking at displays of gleaming kitchen utensils, creamy linen stationary, and lifelike silk flowers. However the real draw was the promise of an appearance by the newly crowned Miss America, who'd won the coveted title less than a week before.

When Emily and I walked past the empty booth advertising Miss America, I wondered if she knew my old friend Smiley.

Seconds later she came striding down the aisle with a bevy of bossy-looking chaperones. So I spontaneously told Emily to hang on a second and walked toward her to see if she did. On the way, a "little white lie" formed in my mind.

I didn't want Miss America to think I was some weird groupie who stalked blondes in tiaras so when she looked up, that lie leapt right off my lips. "Hello, my friend Smiley said if I ran into you here for me to tell you 'Hi' from her." It seemed innocent enough. I rationalized the wee deception instantaneously with the assumption that Smiley probably would have told me to tell her hello. But after I spoke, Miss America's eyes widened and she looked flustered.

I thought, *Uh oh, I guess she doesn't know Smiley after all.*

But then she stammered, "Smiley and I both have … uh … big feet … we're … uh … tall girls … we wear … uh … 10-and-a-half Ds."

I didn't know quite how to respond. I thought, *They really need to give these girls some basic public speaking training before letting them travel all over the world representing America.* When I smiled and replied with a polite comment, I couldn't help but notice that she was still looking at me like a deer in the glare of cement truck headlights. I also noticed that her handlers were whispering anxiously and staring at me. Miss America looked like she was about to cry and asked if I wanted her to sign a picture for me. But by now, the interaction seemed so bizarre that I just wanted to escape, so I said, "No thank you, I really just wanted to tell you that Smiley said 'Hi.' " Then I turned and walked back to toward Emily.

However when I sidled up next to her, Emily demanded, "What in the *world* did you say to Miss America?" and gestured toward her being whisked away by her entourage. I defensively responded, *"All* I said was that Smiley said 'Hi.' " Emily cried, "Oh no!" and covered her mouth with her hand. After a few seconds of horror, she proceeded to inform me about the recent brouhaha regarding the Miss America pageant—which I'd totally missed out on due to a busy week without time for channel surfing.

Evidently Smiley disagreed with the judges' decision and thought *she* should have been crowned the winner. So while the new Miss America was still adjusting her crown, Smiley served up some juicy statements to the national media essentially claiming the contest was rigged. Her sour grape remarks made headlines across the country and were lampooned on late night talk shows for days. Emily reasoned that since the fiasco was still fresh, Miss America must've assumed I was passing along a veiled threat from Smiley. What I thought was an innocuous fib had smacked that poor girl right in the heart!

Ouch! What do you think would Pastor James would have said to me in that moment (see Jas. 1:26)?

OK, I've confessed. How about you? Have you let blessing and cursing come out of your mouth too? (See Jas. 3:6-10.) Want to tell me about it?

Read Psalm 116:2. Do you think God really hears *every single word* that falls out of our mouths? Do you think He also hears every word that runs through our minds? How does the fact that God has perfect hearing make you feel *today?*

The Israelites probably thought their complaints about Yahweh were innocuous too. So when He accuses them of speaking harsh words about Him, they cry out defensively, "What did we say that offended you, Father?"

The clause translated "Your words have been hard against me" in Malachi 3:13 comes from a Hebrew idiom (also found in 2 Samuel 24:4 and 1 Chronicles 21:4), implying the words of the speaker " 'overcome, overpower, overrule' those to whom they are spoken."[4] Of course, the Israelite's words didn't overcome God because He was weak or less adept at arguing anymore than withholding their tithes and offerings left Him unable to pay His rent!

scene three

RESPONSE (FROM GOD):

You have said, "It is vain to serve God. What is the profit of our keeping his charge or of walking as in mourning before the LORD of hosts? And now we call the arrogant blessed. Evildoers not only prosper but they put God to the test and they escape." Malachi 3:14-15

My friend and pastor's wife, Kim Thomas, teaches, "Comparison thinking is a losing battle either way—you either get small or you get smug." Unfortunately, biblical history reveals that Malachi's peers aren't the only ones who struggled with defeatist attitudes. God's people have *always* struggled with comparison thinking.

- Cain compared his responsibilities to Abel's and developed a murderous grudge.
- Sarah compared her lack of maternity wear to Hagar's closet full and banished her to the desert.
- Saul compared the folk songs sung about him to the ones belted out for David and flew into a jealous rage that ended up consuming him.
- Even Asaph—the president of the Old Testament Worship Leader Association—wasn't immune to melancholy I-got-the-short-end-of-the-stick pondering.

"comparison thinking is a losing battle either way—you either get small or you get smug."

Read Psalm 73:1-14. How about you? Have you been feeling small or smug lately?

Have you ever resented other women in church who don't volunteer for as many ministry activities as you do? If so, how did/does the resentment you had/have for ministry-shirkers affect your joy in serving?

What did the people in Isaiah 58:3 complain to God about?

How did God respond to their complaint in Isaiah 58:4-9?

Have you ever observed a religious ritual degenerate into a meaningless formality? If so, describe how.

What's the most repetitious *comparison* question you find yourself asking God?

What's the most repetitious *beneficial* question you find yourself asking God?

scene four

IMPLICATION (FROM GOD):

The LORD paid attention and heard them,
and a book of remembrance was written
before him of those who feared the LORD.
… "They shall be mine, says the LORD of
hosts, in the day when I make up my treasured possession. … For behold, the day is
coming, burning like an oven, when all the
arrogant and all evildoers will be stub-
ble. … But for you who fear my name, the
sun of righteousness shall rise with healing in its wings. You shall go out leaping
like calves from the stall. And you shall
tread down the wicked, for they will be
ashes under the soles of your feet, on the
day when I act, says the LORD of hosts. …
Behold, I will send you Elijah the prophet
before the great and awesome day of the
LORD comes. And he will turn the hearts of
fathers to their children and the hearts
of children to their fathers, lest I come
and strike the land with a decree of utter
destruction." Malachi 3:16b—4:6

Like the shimmering planes of a perfect diamond, our Creator Redeemer's summation speech at the end of Malachi displays four facets.

1. Faithful, postexilic Israelites will launch a revival (3:16a).
2. God will remember those who remain faithful (3:16b-18).
3. The Day of the Lord will serve to both punish the wicked and reward the righteous (4:1-6a).
4. If God's people don't keep their covenant with God, their land will be destroyed (4:6b).

In my opinion the third facet gleams the brightest because of this one verse: "For you who fear my name, the sun of righteousness shall rise with healing in its wings. You shall go out leaping like calves from the stall" (Mal. 4:2).

The first part of this shimmering Scriptural sliver reminds me of a story my friend Laura told me recently. She attended a Christian convention with her husband—who's an author—and described how she wandered aimlessly through the convention center while he was in a publishing meeting. She said she'd begun to feel a little jaded by the commercialism—the booths advertising inspirational self-help books and T-shirts with God slogans—when she caught a glimpse of a man in a flowing white robe and long brown hair a few aisles over. She said at first she was confused by his ancient apparel but then was absolutely compelled forward by the compassionate expression he was wearing. Before she could help herself, she began trotting toward the stranger with her arms outstretched, exclaiming, "Jesus!"

"Wings" are a poetic image for the rays of the "sun of righteousness" (Mal. 4:2). "Malachi's readers probably would have thought this image predicted the sudden appearance of God himself, who is elsewhere compared to the sun (Ps. 84:11; Isa. 60:19-20; … Rev. 21:23). But Christian interpreters throughout the history of the church have understood this prophecy to be fulfilled in Christ, who is 'the light of the world' (John 8:12)."[5]

Of course, Laura's bubble was quickly burst when he intro- duced himself as the actor who simply played the part of Jesus in a recent video Bible project. However, I think her enthusiastic response to a divine doppelganger is a sweet reminder that we *are* going to meet Jesus face-to-face one day! We won't have to trot a few aisles over to reach Him either. Instead the Good Shep- herd will stride toward us with His everlasting arms outstretched. Then He'll bend down and scoop each one of us into His em- brace. And every bruise we've experienced, literally or figuratively, will disappear. The fissures in our broken hearts will close up. The doubt and disappointment in our minds will fade into perfect peace. In that moment, when the *real* Messiah lavishes us with the perfect affection we've been aching for our whole lives, we will be absolutely and completely healed.

I can't wait to be held by Him!

What emotions come to mind when you read the psalm- ist's exclamation about what it will be like when he sees Jesus face-to-face? "As for me, I shall behold your face in righteousness; when I awake, I shall be satisfied with your likeness" (Ps. 17:15).

Describe a time when you were reunited with someone you love after a long separation (maybe when your child came home for the first time after being away at camp or col- lege or when your parent or spouse came home after being deployed overseas in the military). Did you feel satisfied during the reunion? What else did you feel when you finally got to see your loved one face-to-face again?

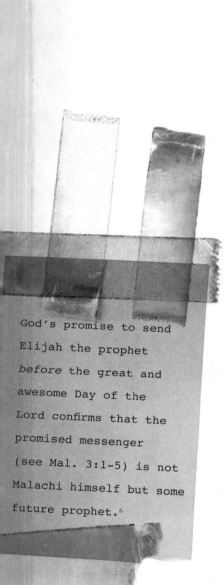

God's promise to send Elijah the prophet *before* the great and awesome Day of the Lord confirms that the promised messenger (see Mal. 3:1-5) is not Malachi himself but some future prophet.[6]

The second half of Malachi's messianic prophecy here in 4:2 really tickles my evangelical funny bone! Granted I'm partial to this phrase because as a motorcycle riding, dancing believer, the boogying cow part resonates with my inner rebel. But even more so I love the imagery of pirouetting livestock because of the joyful freedom it depicts. Which reminds me of another joyful freedom parade I got to participate in a few years ago.

My friend Judy had coerced me into joining her for a 10k road race in downtown Denver. Mind you it took a lot of coercing because I have the runner's equivalent of Attention Deficit Disorder—I find any distance over 3 or 4 miles to be about as pleasant as sticking my hand in a blender! But I love hanging out with Judy, I love the mountains, and this particular race had cute T-shirts, so against my better judgment I agreed to compete.

Of course, I had second thoughts on the morning of the race because it had started snowing—the heavy, wet spring kind—and I'd forgotten to bring a jacket or a fleece. I stood there shivering at the starting line, my forehead creased with worry lines. What if I come in dead last? What if I get hypothermia? What if those really chubby old ladies over there beat me? Then suddenly *Bang!* The starter's pistol rang out and we were off.

For a mile or so I was right up there with the leaders, racing along at breakneck speed, enjoying the roar of the spectators as we flew past. But then the course veered uphill and the cheers of fans faded away. Soon all I could hear was my own ragged breathing. Before the race was even half over, I was scanning for potholes, hoping to twist my ankle so I could hobble off the course with some stolen dignity.

Then suddenly there was a commotion to my right and when I turned to see what it was, I was shocked to discover a giant bacon-lettuce-and-tomato sandwich jogging next to me—not exactly pirouetting livestock but still comically rare! This meal-on-wheels was comprised of three young men, bungee-corded together and wearing huge foam cutouts that had been spray painted to resemble a BLT. The first guy was dressed like a 7-foot-tall piece of Wonder Bread, trailing a very lifelike piece of lettuce-tarp. The second guy was barely visible, with only his face poking through enormous strips of rubber "bacon," which were affixed to a tomato wedge of horror movie proportions. Merrily bringing up the rear was another grinning slice of Wonder Bread, slathered in painted-on mustard. It was the most creative costume I've ever seen at a sporting event, and it was passing me!

However their winks of camaraderie and shouts of encouragement provided just the spark I needed to rise to the occasion and pick up the pace, and pretty soon we were sprinting neck and bread in about 109th and 110th place respectively. I crossed the finish line mere seconds ahead of the snack (I think their wind resistance gave me a slight advantage) and sprawled to the ground in a heap laughing. It had been one great, big, cold, fast, slow, uphill, downhill, hilarious, liberating, glorious adventure!

Which is pretty much God's concluding promise in Malachi. A life devoted to Him will sometimes be cold, sometimes be uphill, and sometimes be not at all what we came prepared for. But with His help we'll rise to the occasion and experience the most glorious adventure possible this side of Heaven!

Reread Malachi 3:16. What do you think the Israelites said when they *spoke* to each other?

How do other believers in your life speak to you in a way that helps you remember God's faithfulness?

What do you think God remembers in His book of remembrance?

What similarities do you think might exist between King Xerxes' honor roll in Esther 6:1-11 that saved Mordecai's neck and the book of remembrance in Malachi 3:16?

In the New Testament we read often about God's Book (see Phil 4:3; Rev 3:5; 13:8; 17:8; 20:12,15; 21:27). How do you suppose these references relate to the book of remembrance in Malachi?

- ❑ same book
- ❑ unrelated book
- ❑ New Testament book is fulfillment of Malachi
- ❑ other (explain)

Here at the end of our study, what would you tell a friend that the Book of Malachi is about?

How would you compare Paul's message in Romans 8:18 to New Testament Christians with Malachi's message to God's people in the Old Testament?

What do you consider the most valuable thing you've learned from Malachi?

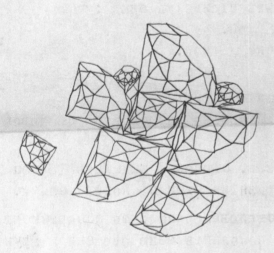

MINING PERSONAL JEWELS FROM MALACHI'S STORY

Plan a reunion within the next month with your *Malachi: A Love That Never Lets Go* small group.